Women Wish
&
Men Dream

By

Paul Henderson

Copyright © Paul Henderson 2023
This book is sold subject to the condition that it shall not, by way of trade or otherwise, be lent, resold, hired out, or otherwise circulated without the publisher's prior consent in any form of binding or cover other than that in which it is published and without a similar condition including this condition being imposed on the subsequent publisher.
The moral right of Paul Henderson has been asserted.

DEDICATION

I would like to give my sincere thanks to every single person who assisted with my research, also my wife and family for the endless amount of time that I was out at these meetings and also for the endless hours spent at the computer.

CONTENTS

ACKNOWLEDGEMENTS i
FOREWORD & DISCLAIMER iii
1. STARTING YOUR JOURNEY 1
2. VAGINA VOODOO OR PENIS POWER 19
3. ABUSIVE RELATIONSHIPS 44
4. RIGHT OR WRONG 78
5. CONSIDERATION & CARE 109
6. UNDERSTANDING 132
7. SEXUAL & STUFF 163
ABOUT THE AUTHOR 180

ACKNOWLEDGEMENTS

To the many people who gave their time to assist me with this information and allowed the sometimes awkward questions.

Foreword & Disclaimer

I welcome you to my book, which has caused me many tongue-in-cheek moments during the research. I would point out that comments and views within this book have been obtained by speaking to those human beings who are lucky enough to still retain a "Sense of Humour" and can think for themselves.

To those people, I thank you for your assistance, humour and straight talking.

I do, however, realise that there are some sad people around who love to shout 'discrimination', 'sexist' or suchlike, as this world has become a place where common sense and people's personal opinions are often a sour pill to swallow.

Therefore, I would like to remind those people that this book and its contents do not wish to offend and comments are from female and male humans, stating their views and opinions and not the personal views of the writer.

If you should feel that this book is not to your taste or you may be offended, then please put the book down now and refrain from reading any further.

I would like to give my sincere thanks to those people in

Frimley and Camberley in Surrey; also, those in Farnborough, Winchester, and Basingstoke in Hampshire who took part in my research for this book, as their support and information were invaluable.

I have one last thing to say to those of you who wish to moan. Just remember, not everyone is as sad as you are.

Get A Life.

Examples and comments throughout this book can be related to both males and females and nothing is used as a sexual smear or to be derogatory toward either sex, and as stated, are comments made during conversation with other male and female humans.

You can't buy a cream for a Seven-Year Itch

Love is a little word; it's people

Who make it big.

(Notes by Joy Edwards)

The following quote was said to me on a hen night:

The older men get, the more childlike, they become.

The average marriage in the UK lasts a little over eleven years.

The most common grounds for divorce are:

Lack of Commitment

Infidelity

Conflict/Arguments

In the UK, the dive accepted grounds for divorce are:

Adultery, Unreasonable Behaviour, Desertion,

Living Apart for 2 Years

And

Living Apart for at least 5 Years.

1. Starting Your Journey

I was told when younger that life is a journey and every journey starts with your very first steps.

But, it seems that from a young age we humans spend most of our lives trying to find those special "Friends". Even as a youngster at school you try to fit into the crowd, but the main problem is just that, "fitting in", as often there are those people who deem themselves superior. Even at a young age they want to be in charge, like those small-minded bullies who feel that they have a right to push everyone around. Problem is that if you do not meet their standards or kiss up to them then you may be out of luck and you could even become one of their targets, forced to hand over your money or sweets, but their actions are never acceptable and in the end it is better to stand up to them, even if you do get another smack from them.

I found out at a young age that these bullies are often the biggest cowards when caught on their own.

As you get older, you meet people who you have contact with through work or simply socialise with, whom at first seem to be nice straightforward people who look and act as if they are friendly towards you, but sometimes you can be so wrong.

The main problem between friends and even family can be jealousy, as it's invisible at first, but after time can grow and become hatred between you and those that you felt a real connection with upon first contact. This is when your friends can become your enemies, if jealousy raises its ugly head you can often find that those friends who seemed to be so genuine are not as you first thought and are often two-faced behind your back.

This, I am sorry to say, is called human nature these days.

Many or most of those friends that you grew up with and who you believed would be with you all of your life, fall away and disappear soon after you leave school, quite often through jealousy or the fact that they were just being two-faced or shallow from the very start to fit into the popular crowd.

This is no loss to you and you need to put it down as the earlier stages in your life that do not matter and move on.

This often happens in our present-day lives as there are endless amounts of people who want to be the centre of attention, as their lives are empty voids and without this spotlight and being the main attraction in the workplace or at any social gathering, they will be nothing but empty, sad people.

They spend their time believing that everyone loves them and that they are an important part of everyone's life, but the truth is that most of these people, who believe that we admire them, are normally dismissed as fools, whilst others who they believe to be their friends do not like them, as they realise that they are two-faced and spend most of their time trying to turn people against each other to make themselves more important.

A group of fifteen women invited me to a hen party so I could hold a question-and-answer session for my book.

Most of the women stated that they had grown apart from their old school friends as they found them the be childish or bitchy, whilst only one woman had stayed in contact with one girl that she went to school with, but stated that they only saw each other occasionally.

When this question was asked at a man's stag night, I was surprised that most of the guys stated that they know and sometimes bump into guys that they went to school with, but have all mostly moved on and cannot be bothered, but enjoyed bumping into some of the girls.

I do not think, therefore, that this defines any clear answers, as it seems to be down to the individual in each case and their preference.

Mobile phones and computers came into many conversations and many people agreed that the more technology expands its reach within mankind, the easier it has become to text and communicate with others, but many made the comment that technology seems to have removed most of the human touch and personal contact that face-to-face conversations maintained, thus life has become more technical and less human. I am sure that most of us are more than aware of this when walking through our daily lives, as many of those people you pass, especially the younger generation groups, have a mobile phone stuck to their hand or earphone in their ears, speaking loudly or playing music.

So how many times do you hear anyone say "good morning" or greet people? Yes, technology has made contact a whole lot easier, whilst removing the personal face-to-face soul of conversations.

Then there is the other side of technology, those who have hundreds of "FRIENDS" on certain sites on the internet, but do not have any real friends in their "life circle". Most people thought that these have to be the saddest in the crowd.

But being friends does not always mean that you are going on holiday together or going to the pub every night; being a friend has many more responsibilities, such as supporting a friend or simply being a voice at the end of the phone in times of need.

But the main problem nowadays is social media, as typing to someone who you have never met or only know through a selection of photographs on a website can be so impersonal, and this was the reason behind so many men and women asking, can it be that society has lost its humanity when lives revolve around "friends" who you only know through a website? Many people also commented on how dangerous this can be in more ways than you know.

After all, how do you know how many of those so-called "online friends" from pictures may even exist as real people? The true question here is, are they the person behind the keyboard?

Another concern with placing so much dependency upon technology is losing human contact which is achieved through face-to-face conversations.

One comment was made about asking for directions from strangers, as it seems that about 90% of the people around you blankly pass you as if unaware that you exist, it is as if you are in another dimension. You are invisible to those passing by you as so many people do not wish to converse with strangers.

Some people commented that they were unsure if this was pure ignorance in some people or if they were simply afraid to make eye contact.

Luckily enough in our present-day society, technology has come to the rescue with online maps and directions, but still removes human interaction.

Talking about technology, it also seems that even dumping a partner is more likely to be done by text message or email nowadays, rather than face-to-face contact. What a cowardly way out.

Some men and women stated that they felt this was often

be the easiest way out of a relationship for them, as breaking up with partners can often turn nasty, whilst men said they felt that as soon as the lady turned the waterworks on, they were at an instant disadvantage and felt pressurised to back down.

So many stated that this is the moment they cave in and feel so bad for the woman that they stay with them, only to find that in a few weeks they are the ones receiving the Dear John.

Strange just how often I have heard this happens.

It could be that the lady feels a lot better if she kicks your arse to the kerb, instead of the other way around, and who can blame her? We guys are often just heartless bastards, so I am told (guess who by).

We all understand that the internet has become a big part of everyday life, but I am sorry to say that it is also an ideal set-up for villains and con merchants to find their next victims.

Many websites offer services such as matchmaking, dating or meeting your soulmate and these seem to be the perfect place to find the man or woman of your dreams, like the millionaire's son or daughter, or the son or daughter of a diamond mine owner, as it is just amazing how many millionaires and their relations use these websites.

Some people on these sites advertise themselves as rich relatives of millionaires or even millionaires themselves, when in fact they are not all they seem and are just dirty crooks waiting to trap their next victim with their stolen lifestyle; a lifestyle that is being paid for by the previous victim they ripped the heart out of whilst emptying their bank account and maxing out their credit cards.

This was carried out without the slightest feeling of remorse. These practices will no doubt continue if you are not wise and staying fully alert.

Yes, there are many genuine people on the internet, but also many scumbag "genuine people" who will sweep you off your feet with well-rehearsed stories of their beautiful lifestyle of fast cars and jetting off to faraway places in the sun, and this, I am sorry to say, is how the most aware people can fall foul of their cons.

Everything they do or say is simply their line to make you fall for them and as soon as you are under their spell, feeling at ease in their company and surroundings, whilst assured that you have hit the jackpot and found the man or woman of your dreams, they will start to pull you in like a fish upon a line.

Now as with any of their previous victims before you, you are being set up as their next money cow. This will happen after a short period, then the sting will begin. It normally starts when their bank has a computer problem or their parents have not paid their allowance, or even that they are waiting to get money in from a sale of property, which should be tomorrow, so can you loan them some money till then?

Yes, they have a boat, a plane, and a Rolls-Royce so how can they need you to loan them cash or the use of a credit card? Come on, stupid, do **NOT** fall for their lies.

YES, this is bullshit as they are out to scam you.

This has become big business and can involve anyone who uses dating sites or simply meets that perfect rich stranger in a bar or nightclub.

This is the person who is flashing the cash and buying drinks to get everyone's attention.

Even if they are caught most of the time they walk free, whilst you are left with maxed-out credit cards and an empty bank account and endless creditors climbing all over you to settle what is **their** balance.

Technology has, I am sorry to say, made it so much easier for con men and women to steal from people by dazzling them with bright shiny things, things that we could not normally afford, and we seem to hear more of this scam every day.

Of course, there are those who use dating sites just for sex, giving the other person hopes of love then after having sex, amazingly, they find that they are not ready for commitment. Scum of the dating sites, but they are everywhere.

So being fully aware and on your guard nowadays is a very good practice to maintain. As the saying goes, "Better to be safe than sorry."

Here are a few steps to follow

Never loan or give money to anyone you meet through a chat room, in a bar, or a club.

Never believe anything anyone tells you or pictures seen on dating sites unless you can prove it for yourself 100%. Remember pictures can be digitally changed.

If someone tells you that they are a millionaire, then tells you that they are having money problems, don't believe a word that they say and say **NO** to loans for them, and never let anyone have the use of your credit cards, no matter how many times they tell you a sob story or that they love you, as this is all part of the trap.

Remember that this type of crime is being used a lot through dating websites, so be very careful.

Otherwise, you could be paying off thousands for someone else's lifestyle, whilst your own is flushed down the toilet, often along with your identity.

If you loan money in any of these situations, then you are the only person that you can blame as there is **NO excuse**

for stupidity and expecting sympathy is just not going to happen.

Please think first, before you regret it.

Another thing to remember is if someone is a bragger, you cannot trust anything that they say so keep these thoughts to yourself. If someone has been born into a rich family, would they really be flashing the cash?

Being careful is not dumb and in the long run, it could save you a lot of cash and upset.

As present-day society is so money orientated, it is no surprise that these corrupt scumbags are always coming up with new cons to trick gullible people out of their money.

Therefore, remembering that so many unsavoury characters have managed to sliver their way out of the sewers knowing that money cons are the easy way to earn cash, and are always on the lookout for those simple, easily led fools in our society, whether it is over the internet, down the pub or in a high-class bar, there is a far greater need to use some common sense when meeting people to assist you to keep safe, both financially and in body and mind, as it is always better to be safe rather than sorry.

Remember that it would be very nice to be born with a built-in bullshit detector, but as humans are not that lucky, you have to go into every life situation with your guard up when meeting new people, and have in the back of your mind the fact that unless you have known someone for some time, then you will not know them at all, and as I stated previously, "people who are loaded keep it to themselves". So next time someone you meet drops into a conversation that they are a diamond mine owner or related to a rich family, just tell them, "Oh yeah, sure." (Think to yourself, *My bullshit detector has just gone off*.)

You also need to take this into account if a friend introduces someone to you and tells you that this person is their new rich boyfriend or girlfriend. (Think to yourself, *I wonder if they are fully aware that they may soon be added to the Victim List*.) The next move is yours; do you say anything or simply be quiet?

Most of these people are so over-charming to a point of being sickly and are often far too sure of themselves, so do not be a sucker for their story.

I was advised by a friend that he has dealt with many of these offenders and always found their types to be total scum with no heart or concern for any of their victims, and suggested that the best way to catch them out is by simply sitting back and dropping a few bait words into a conversation. You often find that this is a great way of showing whether the person that you are talking to is genuine or not.

A good bait is to mention that a member of your family

has passed away, who may I add was very well off financially. Their ears will prick up and you will find the conversation moving over to that subject, sometime soon.

Yes, I realise it is a bit sick, but it is amazing how the tables can be turned and you can soon get an idea of how much this person is money hunting. This is why it is always solid ground to get to know someone over time and not just jump into the sack with them upon the first date, as so many people do nowadays.

I am fully aware that this is totally down to the individual but remember, these are the views of many people interviewed and not of the writer, as I can assure you, I too, fell for this before.

Life can be a wonderful happy place, but it all depends on you. Not everyone's life will turn out as they wished; sometimes friendships and relationships are pretty much the same, and you don't always get back what you put into them.

So don't blame others if your relationship or life fails to turn out how you wanted it to be, as it could have been caused by one of two reasons.

It could simply be that you or your partner have not put enough effort into your relationship, or it is as simple as you are not suited, but if you spend your life sat upon your arse doing nothing about it then you only have yourself to blame. If you have nothing to show for your years upon this planet then it is your own fault. Do something about it before it is too late, as so many people believe that life should come to them.

Showing someone who you are in a relationship, with that you care for or love them, is not a weakness and can be a blessing, especially when the same feelings are reciprocated, but what we have to remember is that treating someone fairly and respectfully, whilst taking into account their feelings, does not mean that you are wasting your time. If you should feel that you are in a loveless relationship, then it is down to you to make up your own mind to stay or go.

Sometimes certain people will stay in a relationship for financial security or gain as their partner works and pays the bills or has money, whilst they remain at home watching the television or sleeping the day away, often giving endless excuses as to why they cannot get a job, but mostly it is because they know that they have a good thing going.

Yes, it can be very hard to walk away from any relationship if you feel a strong bond with the other person, but ask yourself this: what has the other person put into your relationship? If the answer is nothing then you have answered your own question. On the other hand, if they have taken care of your children, cooked, cleaned, done the washing, what else do you want?

If you have gone to work and come home to a meal on the table and a clean house and all your washing and ironing done, then stop frigging moaning and be grateful, as a maid would cost you a hell of a lot more, now show some consideration.

Often in some relationships, it can seem that both the male and the female are as hard as each other to communicate with or understand, as both have their faults and they blame each other for their relationship problems, whilst refusing to communicate with each other over those problems.

Humans are a strange bunch of creatures who instead of striving for a happy, loving partnership and life, seem to spend most of their time arguing or trying to kill each other.

Of course there are other problems such as being shallow, as this will not help in any relationship.

I am sad to say that in today's society there are endless amounts of males and females who think that they are so beautiful that they can have anyone they wish, but being involved with these people does put a lot of strain upon a relationships, as they love themselves more than their partner.

Just imagine what it would be like if both partners were like this, as they would be fighting over the mirror, makeup or hairdryer.

Many of the human race are unable to communicate with each other due to being afraid of disappointing or offending others, which is even more prevalent in this present time. This often seems to be the reason life is a continual disappointment to many people, who feel like every day is made up of continual work, work, work, or that the world owes them something.

We all understand that the stress of everyday life places a lot of pressure upon family life and relationships, and this is the main reason so many people have become blinkered towards enjoying their weekends.

Life seems to push some couples to the verge of breaking point due to the stress it causes to family life. Other causes are a bereavement in the family, where one partner has been left property or valuables by a relation and the other partner feels that they have a right to share.

Often what some people think would be of help financially, turns into a cause for arguments.

But I must point out that this is not the same in every case, as security can often change a relationship and bring about a stronger footing for the couple to move on with their life together, but money does not always bring happiness.

If, say, you have gone through a lot of stress looking after a family member who is old or suffering from an illness such as dementia, you could find that this sort of situation can take its toll upon your relationship. Then this can do one of two things: either make you stronger together or break your relationship apart due to the arguments and built-up stress that has come between you, especially if the person you were looking after was one of your parents.

For anyone who is caring for an elderly relative, it is hard enough watching your parent dissolve into an empty shell right in front of you, whilst your partner tells you that they should put them into a home. This can be so soul-destroying that all you feel is total resentment for your partner. You feel that comments that are not what you wish to hear, even if they could be right in the end, at that moment can make you both question whether you should stay together or not.

The thing that you must take into consideration is the fact that your partner has been with you all through this hell, standing by your side and keeping you together. If they are the type who just left you to deal with it alone then tell them to get lost; as your partner they should be supporting you.

Now, men, think of this. You sitting down at home spending time having a well-earned rest, as we think.

Then the lady of the house comes in and tells you that you could be doing some of the well-needed jobs around the house.

We men always believe that every time we sit down the wife/partner has something for us to do.

But think of it another way.

Your partner could have spent hours doing the jobs around the house that so many of us men deem as "women's work", when in fact these jobs should be classed as family tasks, as any member of a family is able to use a hoover or wash up.

Teaching your husband/wife and children to clean up after themselves makes life a lot easier for all.

So, with this in mind, sometimes it is a lot easier for guys and girls to remember that a relationship is not a way to replace your mother, who was the person who used to clean up after you when you lived at home with your parents.

This is not always the case, as I have known parents who were slobs and expected someone else to clean for them.

Consideration goes a very long way in any relationship, such as a simple task like taking a plate or cup out to the kitchen and placing it into the dishwasher, instead of expecting your partner to wait upon you like a maid.

Or putting the dustbins out for collection, as this is often left to the other partner.

This was just a couple of complaints that I picked up upon, so consideration is another good practice within a relationship.

Remember: marriage is not an excuse to turn your partner into a maid.

Ways to kill a relationship dead

Infidelity

Money Worries

Jealousy

Abusiveness

Got Married Too Young or Too Fast

Drug Use

Sexual Incompatibility

Always Arguing

Not Forgiving

No Compromise

Unrealistic Expectations

Lack of Empathy

Getting Together for the Wrong Reasons

No Respect

Lack of Communication

Constant Condescending Attitude

Unwanted Pregnancy

2. Vagina Voodoo or Penis Power

Men often say, "You can't live with them and you can't live without them." What are they talking about? Why, women, of course, and this attitude is why so many of us bring about our demise within relationships, as we act more like primates.

When I told some women about this comment, their reply was plain and simple. "We don't know why we waste our time as men never listen and always refuse to accept any of the faults are their own doing."

Men say that women have to be the greatest mystery known to man. These wonderful, and often frustrating creatures can be your best friends one moment and your arch-enemies the next.

Being a man and keeping a woman happy often depends upon just how good the man is at keeping his mouth shut and refraining from saying what is really upon his mind (or simply doing as he is told).

This, as we all know, is something that we men are not able to do, thus causing many of the underlying problems in our relationships, those which are normally brought about by males failing to consider that a woman is a human being with feelings, emotions and their own opinion, which you will no doubt learn about over time together.

It does not matter how much a man loves a woman, he may sometimes think that she is the most infuriating part of his life. Whilst a woman will simply think, *Why in hell were men invented in the first place if it were not to upset women?* But would they want to be without each other? Well, only sometimes depending on the mood.

Yes, we men lay most of the blame at the feet of our ladies, but is it fair to do so, or are they the innocent parties here and it's we men who cause the problems in the first instant, like most women often accuse us of and we are just passing the buck?

Well, this simply depends on your point of view at this early stage.

Surprisingly, both men and women have their personal views, after all, they are both humans. Yes, guys, our ladies often think for themselves. Even though many men think and act like they are the superior beings on this planet, in fact some act more like primates, than humans.

This is where our problems begin. Whilst disagreements within relationships will always be part of living and loving each other, there will always be ways to act and treat each other to make your journey along the romance highway less bumpy.

Men, please remember the days of whacking someone around the head and dragging them back to your cave have long gone.

Women want to be treated with respect and shown love, and why not? It could cost you a bunch of flowers or a box of chocolates every so often, but in the end, it could be worth it. Just think of the rewards that you could receive in return. Wink, wink. (I must, however, point out that there are many cases where roles may be reversed in this situation.)

We humans need to be aware and have a certain level of understanding that for humans to live together for any long period and expect perfect harmony, they need to work together and be able to communicate.

Friendships are normally quite easy to manage as you do not spend every day together, whilst relationships and marriage are on a completely different level, as often one or both partners fight to be the dominant one, which can cause friction.

This is where learning to talk to each other without moaning each time you have a conversation can make your life together a whole lot easier.

Amazing as it may seem, it is not always the women who do all of the moaning, as many of us men are fully aware that we are moaners (myself included). Quite often this is simply because you feel that life has not turned out the way you wanted it to be, but whose fault is that? Most of our lives held visions of riding off into the sunset with a sexy woman upon a Harley-Davidson. (Sorry, dreaming for a moment there.)

Life, I am sorry to say, is not as you see it in the movies and not everything turns out all roses in the end, but working together, building trust and loving each other whilst being able to open up to each other about your concerns and worries, is a strong start to building a healthy bond in any relationship.

A loving word every so often also helps as well and remember, boys, the saying, "Happy Wife, Happy Life," this does work both ways, as often in relationships couples get too comfortable and fail to keep the love fire burning.

Respecting someone, whilst loving them, is also a good bond in any relationship, even if they moan at you occasionally, as the fun is in kissing and making up.

Taking the time to sit down with a coffee or whatever and talk to each other about how you feel is an easier way to solve a problem and can promote trust between you even if you were both considering breaking up. Always remember that a relationship that falls apart is only good for solicitors to take lots of your money from you.

I would, however, never suggest confiding in friends or work colleagues before speaking with your partners, as friends and those you work with are often not as closed-mouthed as you think, or will sometimes use your problems to get their agenda underway. This is often how affairs start, as those that you tell can use your situation against you.

One of the main problems of life is a lack of dedication in relationships, as in previous generations couples were often real partnerships and mostly dedicated to each other and worked together, but nowadays it seems that as soon as the wedding day is over couples seem to drift apart and many fail to be concerned about issues as they are just shallow and far too self-opinionated to be able to solve problems within the family circle. Instead they have greater concern as to the car they drive and the false front that they show to others in their posh designer labels.

Men and women always seem to moan about each other but spend so much time looking for another partner if they break up with the last one – crazy.

Many people cannot control their lives and seem to be steamrolled by day-to-day life as the need to impress is so high.

Be yourself, as there are so many plastic people who have to put a false front on.

Now, impressing on your first date is important and depends upon many things. If you take a lady out somewhere that she dislikes then that will more than likely be your first and last date.

So why not be open with her and ask if there is anywhere special she would like to go. If so, ask her if she would like to go to a nice restaurant and whether she has any preferences.

Then you will get some idea as to:

1. The type of food she likes,
2. If she has expensive taste,
3. If she is a freeloader.

If it's no. 2, she may be someone who dates for a free expensive dinner.

If not, speaking charmingly and remembering that she is more than likely feeling as nervous as you are and being open with her, can make you both relax.

Try to get her to open up about herself, her job, her hobbies, and the things she likes. But remember, do not start talking about yourself as there is a good chance that she will not be interested.

Remember, No BS, as she will find out in the end and if she is a nice person you could lose her.

Note to Men: Occasionally, if you may find yourself having a heated conversation with your partner and she brings something up from the past that you do not remember in the same context as she states, at this point, I would simply suggest you just agree and keep quiet.

You may even think that you should tell her she is wrong (that is, if you like living dangerously), but if you are considering that this will be an easy way out, don't, as this will only make matters worse and add fuel to the fire. Simply act dumb and just agree, which may come naturally to some of us guys. And remember, this role can be reversed.

Note

Women must remember that equal opportunities were introduced so that this is not solely a man's world, and to give women the chance to prove to themselves their equality to men, but some men still hold them back as much as possible in many situations.

Question

Why is it that so many women and men nowadays are unable to change a tyre when they get a flat? Is it that society is far too mollycoddled?

Why is it that when men first meet a woman they act like the blood has drained from their brain to their penis?

Quote

When a woman says she loves the simple things in life, why does she always look at her husband?

Every woman is in some way different from the next and a man will find this out in one way or another soon enough.

He may sometimes feel like she is impossible to please, whilst other times she may be a dream to live with (most of the time), but I am informed that these dream ladies are one in a million, as some women pointed out, simply because their partner is useless at reading the hints that she gives him.

Knowing a woman is one thing, loving her is a completely different thing, but understanding her, well, most men believe that is right out there with the other Seven Wonders of the World.

The thing is that it does not matter if a man cannot understand his partner's behaviour, as it is more than likely his fault in the first place, or the fact that a woman can tie a man up in knots whenever she wishes to. What does matter is showing that you care and trying to work together.

Surely, the main reason why a woman can tie a man up in knots is that she has always had the right equipment to confuse the male population throughout history, and will continue to do so as long as males sit upon their thumbs and expect the answer to come to us.

Maybe it is because we men are just simple souls, whose heads are turned by the slightest sight of a breast or a piece of arse, simply because we think with our "private parts". Maybe it is as simple as that.

We men should, however, question ourselves and ask

whether it is our misguided manhood or just plain old being dumb that causes us to suffer so many problems when we become involved with these loving, caring and often confusing members of the opposite sex.

The word to take notice of here is simply "opposite", as women are nothing like men and also nothing like each other. Most are individuals and more often more like their mothers than their friends.

Thinking that women are all the same is the biggest mistake that most men can make and this is where the confusion starts, as we often place all women in the same category. And remember, there is no such thing as "women are all the same".

Most of the problems suffered throughout a man's life are understandable in one way or another, as most come about by our stubbornness or our failure to listen, so I am informed.

Many women that I have spoken to have suggested that if men could understand where they normally go wrong then it would place them in a better position for solving those problems concerning the ladies in their lives, which I feel does seem logical.

Unfortunately, we men know that this cannot always be the case, as any situation relating to a woman in a man's life, or vice versa, becomes extremely difficult to understand, let alone solve, as men feel that the lady in our life often changes her mind, just when we feel that we have sorted the matter out.

Yes, men are fully aware that female-related problems will never have an easy resolution due to the weird and wonderful way that we men think a woman's mind works, but I have come to understand that this is a result of the total lack of understanding that we men have concerning the female population, therefore is it fair for a man to place all of the blame upon a woman for his own shortcomings? Most men will answer, "Well, yes." After all, why should we men blame ourselves? I am, yet again, informed this is normally the way that we men seem to grasp the reality of any situation.

I am also informed that the problem within many relationships is that men are far more open about their hang-ups, feelings and problems. For example, a guy is more likely to say if he has any problems in the bedroom, whereas the lady is less likely to openly admit to this.

Some women do not have the same sex drive as others and some women are not open to experimenting. A few men commented about this subject and said that this can sometimes be a stumbling point in relationships.

There are certain times when many women do not wish to entertain foreplay or sex due to monthly cycles or stress in their lives, and a man needs to show some consideration during these times. Also many women stated that a man must realise that a woman loves sex when it is a caring, emotional act between two people, but do not enjoy it when it is a "personal relief" upon the man's behalf, or a quick wham bam, thank you, ma'am.

There are also many other areas of lovemaking where women suggested men could improve their game and therefore improve their partner's satisfaction, starting with foreplay, as many women said that some men go at this like they are stoking a fire, instead of smooth, soft hand movements to bring your lady to a level of extreme pleasure. As some women are quite easy to warm up, it would allow this to be quite enjoyable for them and therefore not all one-sided.

Some women can also suffer from dryness and this will cause pain when making love, so you guys need to be aware and use lubricants to assist entry. This will also show your partner that you are a caring, thoughtful lover. Another thing is that talking to each other about your likes and dislikes can greatly improve your lovemaking.

Bedroom entertainment can be a bust or a blast and I am told by many women that it is mostly down to the man proving his worth and giving the lady an enjoyable time, but if your partner is just lying there like a corpse then there is no wonder that the guy loses interest and looks elsewhere, as sex is not one-sided, especially if your partner just can't be bothered, then who can blame the other partner for moving on? After all, a person can only stand so much of "I have lost the enthusiasm," or, "I just don't want to," week after week, month after month.

Often lovemaking is all about taking your time and getting it right, as an early ejaculation can be an instant failure, and this can often happen if alcohol is added to the event.

Alcohol can be the cause of Brewer's Droop. This is when the guy gets an erection, but is unable to maintain it due to the amount he has drunk, so try to remember, guys, that if you are on a promise, holding off on the alcohol can often help you perform better.

Lack of interest sometimes happens if you are not enthusiastic about the person that you are with or you suffer from low testosterone. Many men and women suffer from this problem later on in years and there is no shame in seeing a doctor about a lack of enthusiasm (wink, wink) and this can often be an easy fix.

So now we realise that women are different from men, in their moods and chain of thought, along with the wrongs and rights of keeping upon the right side of a woman. Whilst men, instead of solving a problem, it seems that we simply make matters worse by speaking when we should keep quiet, therefore our failure to do what is right just gets us in even more trouble in the end.

This is because we men are experts at opening our mouths without thinking first. This is often why we have so many problems when dealing with the female population, as most women have little interest in a man's opinion in day-to-day life and this becomes even more apparent when you are in a long-term relationship or married.

We men find ourselves pulling our hair out with frustration, whilst the women in our lives carry on moaning at us for a problem that she says we have caused (normally that we do not listen). Even if we believe that it was her fault in the first instance, we will still get the blame for it. (Those of you who are married will know this to be true.) Maybe this is why so many men lose their hair after being married for years.

Now this is where it becomes complicated. If by chance you dare to suggest a solution to a problem, your lady will then change her mind and accuse you of not wanting to listen. Afterwards, their normal put-down to us men is that listening would mean putting ourselves out. It seems that we cannot do anything right.

It is every man's dream to gain the satisfaction of being able to understand the workings of the female mind and what makes them tick, but most of the time we men make any situation worse.

What makes it even more frustrating is when someone says, "You're wasting your time, you'll never understand a woman." This answer is normally given by some fool who has personally failed to find a suitable resolution to a similar situation and then wimped out or ran away.

A few women suggested that a change in the book title was in order, renaming it, 'Men: the Puzzle' or simply, 'The Fools We Date', thus showing that they blame the men in their lives, for most things.

Many of us men are frustrated when dealing with the ladies in our lives and most ladies believe this is due to a basic lack of understanding, but some men are still determined to carry on their search for the knowledge that will someday unravel the infuriating workings of the female mind, thus allowing us to continue some sort of peaceful existence alongside them without being accused of "screwing everything up".

Unless, of course, men move into the garage as a safe zone away from the wife, at which point the women will be cheering and having a party. Many men are still looking for a house where they can have a den or man cave.

Sorry to say, but nobody has as yet come up with all the answers to every question concerning relationships, but we continue to look for some sort of resolution so we can achieve a certain level of male happiness in this world, a place where women will not always have the last and final word in every conversation or disagreement. Some hope.

I have found that most men and women were quite forthcoming in a crowd, but quite unapproachable when by themselves. Many worried that their identity would be disclosed in the book, but became more open and relaxed when I confirmed that no personal information would be published.

As men know, there is nothing worse than having a feeling

of total uselessness in a relationship, as you feel that you're told what to wear, say, or do by your partner. This can often be the case and it is not always the lady who is at fault.

During my research, I have met many women who said that in their relationship it is their man who acts like the woman, so a reversal of roles.

On the other hand, is it unreasonable for a man to expect a woman to accept responsibility and openly admit that she is wrong if a guy will not do the same? Or is it that our ladies are capable of taking any situation and turning it around so it works in their favour? Whilst some men stated that they do not stand a chance in an argument with their partners as men have not as yet grasped the concept of how women achieve this manoeuvre, we are, however, fully aware that it will, unfortunately, work against us in some way or another.

In most situations, men have come to realise that it does not matter how hard we try to conclude a situation. We will generally end up being blamed for causing the problem in the first place. Yet again, we are the ones who are in the wrong and normally apologising for something that we feel we are completely innocent of (or so we think).

However, you would think that as this happens so often throughout a man's lifetime, we should have fully grasped the fact and therefore been ready when this situation recurred, but we never are, and this is why our ladies get the upper hand every time.

This is also why women believe that men often act like little boys when they can't get things to go their way.

Most times, men seem to be completely unaware that they have faults, and these faults are regularly pointed out by the women in our lives, but should you ever try to inform your lady of her faults then be careful, as you may well live to regret it.

Women seem to be good at telling us men that if we were to accept responsibility for our actions, then this is a good way to solve the problems. Yet another idea that only works one way.

Whilst researching for this book, I found that both males and females can often follow the same line of thought when dealing with similar situations. Many comments were made relating to sex and their views on being attracted to a member of the opposite sex upon the first contact, even dreaming of spending some horizontal fun time with them at the first opportunity, and it was not always the men who gave the crudest replies to questions that were asked. I found that some women's replies could be quite blue when the question of a man was involved, especially when it was a crowd of women together. Often their replies were a lot cruder than a crowd of men, and upon one occasion a group of women suggested that if a man had an on/off switch upon his penis then the ladies could use him and then pack him away afterwards with no need for conversation. This, may I add, is called a vibrator.

Conversations that I held with men highlighted one major grievance that most men had with their partners, and this was the number of times a woman can say, "You just don't care," or, "You just don't understand."

For example, your lady gets upset and you ask her what is wrong, at which point she refuses to tell you, stating that she has told you before upon many occasions and by repeating herself would simply be wasting her time, as you do not listen.

Later, she will moan that you did not try to find out. Now think back and I am sure you will remember that you had asked her repeatedly earlier (just before you gave up and walked away), but she will have conveniently forgotten this fact.

I have been informed that the right thing to do in this situation is sit down and comfort your lady, and by doing this show her that you care.

As simple as that, but as we men tend to think that women are making a fuss about nothing most of the time, we ignore them and therefore we would not consider that a resolution to this matter would be as simple as placing your arm around her.

Therefore, with this in mind you can understand why men have been confused about the workings of the female mind for centuries. This is why men always end up concluding that the woman's mind is incapable of working in any logical format whatsoever.

This matter is shown at its best when a man asks a woman a question that he would like to get a straightforward yes-or-no answer to, as on most occasions you will find that a simple "yes or no" reply is just not possible with most women. Be warned, many questions will end up as a full-blown debate lasting sometimes for hours, leaving you confused and unsure as to what the original question was about.

This is why males concluded long ago that the longer we are involved with a woman, the surer we become that trying to decipher the female mind will be the death of us.

Speaking from experience, the worst time to ask your partner a yes-or-no question is just before you attempt to retire for the night, as you will find yourself lying there hours later trying to decipher her unrelated reply, whilst your partner has fallen into a deep sleep hours before.

Many women have informed me that the reason why women tend to debate a question is very simple to answer. "Women have far more sophisticated ways of reasoning than a man."

There is a good probability that this is one of the reasons why after a few years of marriage, most men try to avoid becoming involved in any form of debate with their wives or partners. When married you can often find yourself in situations where you are afraid to give an answer, which is in your head at that particular moment, to a certain question, like, "Does this dress make me look fat?" or, "Do

I look good in this colour?"

Oh my god. This can cause a man to suffer palpitations, sitting there thinking, *Oh shit, what can I say that will not put me in the doghouse?* This is another 'No-Win Situation' and no matter what answer you give, it will be a wrong one.

There are only two ways forward in this situation: you can simply bite the bullet and just say, "No, love, you look lovely," to which your lady will reply that she does not agree with you. Or, you can simply make-believe that you did not hear her, and as women are always moaning that we never listen to them this is a perfect time to use her statement to your advantage. In the end, your comeback can be a simple, "Sorry, love, I was miles away."

At which point she will moan and say the normal, "You never listen." OK, so what's new?

Don't get me wrong, as there are many relationships where the man and woman can communicate in an adult manner and therefore this situation may not occur, but a man has to understand that when he is in a relationship he will be the last person to know what is going on around him, and the truth is that quite often the longer you are in that relationship, the more this deterioration of communication will take place. You can be sure that the situation will become worse over time and this is not helped by periods when we ignore our ladies when they are talking to us.

Also, it is amazing how often I have been told about one

partner moving something, and then accusing the other of moving it, only to find it. Often happens.

We are all fully aware that some relationships suffer from breakdowns, some simply caused by friction between partners whilst sometimes the friction can be a signal of further upset ahead or a possible split. Often there are clear signs along the way long before the end. Some are caused by outside interference or by something very stupid.

One of the worst things that a partner can do is criticise the other partner during this decline as you can guarantee they will live to regret it in so many different ways. If a partner can reuse your comments against you to nail you to the financial wall then they will do so.

Another thing is that women seem to have the view that we men are only capable of thinking of two things: 'football and sex'.

Research can prove that they are wrong as most of the time the male line of thought covers many other areas of interest such as beer, cars, fishing, gardening, porn movies and a whole lot more. All this is going on inside our heads so how can women say that we do not think? It is quite amazing that our daily thought capacity can maintain this sort of flow and experts say that we are still capable of thinking about sex every seven seconds. So guys, pat yourselves on the back for this amazing feat as being able to master such a mental achievement as this in our normal day-to-day life shows that we men are nothing short of being mental geniuses (of course women will disagree with this). Many women believe we men are incapable of carrying out the simplest of tasks, let alone using our brains.

But take some advice: remember, allowing your lady to think she is right does allow you a certain level of peace in the family home, but of course, that will come back to haunt you shortly as it is amazing how our ladies manage to remind us of the fact that they have proved us wrong before, many times.

If you ever contemplate thinking that you have won that discussion, think again, as I can assure you she was only lulling you into a false sense of achievement and will no doubt hit you with another reminder later. This is the reason most of us men walk around in our small world as the wife has confused us so much we retreat into this inner self.

Of course, there will be times when both sexes feel like giving up in their relationship as it feels as if you are getting nowhere, especially if your partner seems to moan endlessly about everything and criticises you over the smallest of things. Often married life can be like this, as spending every day of your life with the same person is bound to wear thin during some periods and if you add children to this equation then it is enough to push a saint over the edge.

Many women made this same comment during my research and also added the following:

Would men be so enthusiastic about making babies if it were the man who had to carry the child inside them for nine months and then go through the pain of delivery?

There were many other comments that men/women mentioned that pissed them off (these words are as I was told):

The Men/Women who create a bullshit past of their career or life to impress.

The Men/Women who know everything, and when proved wrong make excuses.

The Man/Woman who does not buy a drink, but will grab one when someone else is paying.

The Men/Women who believe they are brilliant lovers, but the truth is they are rubbish in the bedroom.

The Men/Women who keep you waiting for ages then say nothing, when they are finally ready.

The Man/Woman who spends all their time talking about past relationships, then mentions they are still married.

The Men/Women who ask you out for a meal then when it is time to pay say they left their wallet at home.

The Men/Women who arrange to go out and then go out with their mates without telling you. When you try to call they do not answer.

The Men/Women who tell you that they love you at the

first kiss goodnight.

The Men/Women who spend all the first dates talking about politics and what the government is doing wrong.

The Men/Women who talk about all of their favourite sex positions and then ask you, what yours is.

The worst are those who give people the come-on then disappoint them just to feel big.

I must add that there were many more that men/women who told me about that happening during their first dates, but some were too worrying to print.

This is one of my favourites.

One woman told me that she went out with a guy (no name) and when she asked him what he did for a job, he replied, "Oh, nothing much."

She thought, *What a boring sod*, and could not wait for the evening to end, but by the end of their evening, she found that the guy was nice and decided to give him another chance and went out on quite a few dates afterwards.

Three weeks later he asked her to pick him up from work so that they could go for drinks and a meal. He told her that a pass would be at the gate and gave her an address.

When she arrived at the address there were lots of security and she was given her pass and told where to park and directions to his building.

She entered and drove to the large white building and parked.

Just as she stopped, the guy walked out to her car and opened the door, whilst he was dressed in a dinner suit, which she thought was odd. Overdressed, but handsome.

He took her by the hand and said, "Come along, I will show you one of my places of work."

He took her inside the building, which was a massive warehouse, and down a long corridor. When she finally got inside the main area he told her, "This is it," and pointed to a film set.

She found out at that moment, he was a stuntman double for a certain film star.

I am unsure of which one as she would not tell me, but she did tell me that she is still with the guy and that was around 10 years ago.

So this proves that until you get to know someone, which takes time, you will not fully understand them. This lady realised that this was why he did not brag, as he was the real deal and... Not Just A Wannabe.

So remember, if you meet someone and they start shouting that they do this or that, you can be sure that in the end, you will learn the truth.

People who do the real job – Don't Shout About It.

Quote

A wife will always forgive and forget, but she will never let you forget that she forgave and forgot.

3. Abusive Relationships Narcissistic Behaviour, Coercive Control & Blind Justice

You may say, "What is Narcissistic Behaviour and Coercive Control?"

Well, let me explain.

Meeting someone can often be a game of chance. At first you will never really know what the person is truly like or if they are hiding their true personality to fool you into a false sense of security.

Simply explained, you meet a person who looks and acts like a nice human being, they ask you out on a date, they flash some cash around or own a nice car and treat you well.

You may think to yourself that at long last a genuinely nice person has walked into your life, or maybe you are fooled by their actions.

This is the way these animals work, selling a false image to their next victim.

Over a period of time you are getting to know them, but you get an odd feeling that all is not what it seems, then after a short time the monster behind the mask becomes more visible.

This person, male or female, could be suffering from NPD or Narcissistic Personality Disorder, which can affect both men and women.

Narcissists can often be extremely dangerous to be in a relationship with as their mood can change in a split second, as if they live in a twilight world of their own self-importance, with a personal view of believing themselves to be superior to everyone they come into contact with at their work or leisure and holding amazing skill to be able to manipulate or lie their way out of any situation.

Narcissists are experts at misleading others, like those in authority, into believing that they are the nicest, most caring people that they will ever meet, a great parent and an honest individual.

However, this is so far from the truth, as their sense of self-importance and survival is so far magnified that it is inflated to levels where they view themselves as god-like compared to others around them and live to gain vengeance should you ever upset them. This can also mean should you ever prove them wrong.

Their need for the admiration of others and the attention of those around them to admire their actions and achievements is obsessive to the point of sometimes being childlike and life-threatening to their partners, and it is nearly impossible to prove they suffer from a narcissistic personality disorder as they will never undertake any form of examination or view to seek therapy.

Aggressive undertones are quite often part of the persona of these types of people and by taking all this into account, and the fact that they will at some point become controlling, abusive and even violent, you could well compare them to having a Jekyll-and-Hyde personality.

The thing about narcissistic people is that their lives as sick individuals is at first contact totally invisible, as they look and act perfectly normal and in fact can often come across like real caring human beings, but the very moment they are upset they turn your life into a Living Hell, as they lack any rational thought or concern for anyone other than themselves, believing that "They" are special and right in every way "<u>Always</u>".

They will cheat and when caught they will blame it upon their partner. "Yes, it is all your doing." And each and every time they will turn every situation around to blame you, as they are far too perfect to be wrong, whilst incapable of feeling remorse or showing true sympathy towards anyone they hurt, adult or child.

This will include any persons who they have harmed, as they will continue to do whatever they can to dominate, control and if need be destroy them through any means possible.

The problem is that you will not normally have a clue that they are narcissistic individuals until it is too late, by which time they have already taken control over your life and often finances, that is, unless you are one of the lucky ones, then I suggest you cut your losses and get the hell out of there, change your mobile number and even move as the outcome can be quite dangerous in some cases. I have heard of partners being beaten, stabbed or even murdered.

There are many other cases where these assaults can be very damaging to the person who becomes involved with these people, as your life can be in ruins as soon as they get control over you, and when you realise what they are like and break up with them, the anger rises to the surface and all the threats start and will continue until you can move well away from them.

Narcissistic individuals tend to get attached quickly in an immature, childish manner and become clingy. Also they are often very good at putting on a front as a passionate loving person. The other side of these sick individuals is that if you watch closely, you see certain times when the nasty side of their behaviour comes to the surface, often aggressive and rude to people in day-to-day life.

These are often the types who are on top form at putting

people down for the simplest of reasons, so be watchful if you take one out to a restaurant or bar.

Narcissistic individuals often become dominant in their relationship very quickly and start to control their partners by belittling, demanding respect, and introducing financial control over them, then overpowering them in every way in an extremely short period, often with extreme effect on their partner's health.

They demand that you stop contact with friends and family who they feel could damage their control over their partner. Also they become extremely irate should you happen to try to speak whilst they are talking, as they love to hear their own voice. This is normally shouted at you as, "I'm speaking!" like a Sergeant Major upon a parade ground.

I know of one such spineless male (Basingstoke area in Hampshire, England) who thinks that he is a real lady charmer, but the only skill this NPD person has is finding himself lonely or unhappy women who are divorced/separated with children and may even own their own property, so he can build his fabrication totally upon a base of lies and bullshit.

He then gives them a story of being high up in a company and earning a very good wage as his first move to get them interested. Then he will work his way into their bed and start to build a visible "Happy Family" scenario so she feels at ease with him, so when he gets access to his child or children, it means that they have other children to play with, plus he has a built-in childcare service should he need it.

IF the lady owns her own property, he will try to manipulate her to sell it and allow him to invest that cash into a money-making scheme, or should I say scam, as the only person who profits will be him.

This is all part of his plan, so to the outside world he is a top caring parent, which is such a load of BS, as everything he does is to make himself look good to those around him and normally believed by those who are too stupid to see through him.

But in reality, the real truth is that the only thing he cares about is himself and that he continues to keep access to his child to maintain control over his ex-partner, whilst using it to build his credibility with the court services and others, and this is what narcissists do.

Their manipulation and deceptions are now complete and as far as outsiders and their new partner are concerned, they are a happy family unit.

That is until the narcissist shows their true personality to yet another partner, which is inevitable, and until then the partner will be totally unaware of what danger they have allowed themself and their children to be placed into. By which time the narcissist will have taken total control of their partner's life, who will be so afraid of him or her that they spend their time around them walking upon eggshells so as not to upset the narcissist.

That is unless they are wise and realised that this spineless creep is only fit to bully, beat or mentally abuse those who become involved with them.

You can tell that a narcissist is a coward as they normally build a security wall around themselves with cameras to keep safe from past victims or their families.

There have been many people that I have come into contact with whilst researching this book, mostly women, who have had previous contact with a person like this, and stated that it is as if I were writing their own story, whilst others have suffered at the hands of these cowardly/sick people through assaults and beatings.

Still, these sick individuals are allowed to continue their abuse whilst family courts and judges in Hampshire and other areas around this country ignore these dangerous individuals and their behaviour by seemingly giving a free pass so they can continue to gain access to their victims and children.

So it seems that they are ignoring the safety and rights of the victim of abuse and their children.

Coercive Control is against the law in the UK, thanks to the endless work of those members of Women's Aid and others, but it seems that many courts and some district judges ignore this fact.

Now there is "**Clare's Law**", often known officially as a

Domestic Violence Disclosure Scheme, which came into being to assist people who have concerns about their partners having violence in their past.

It is always better to be safe than sorry, as you cannot guarantee that family courts will listen.

The project was named after Clare Wood, who was murdered by her ex-boyfriend who had a record of violence:

https://clearcheck.co.uk/can-i-do-a-dbs-check-on-my-partner/

So, if you have any doubts, the quicker you check that person out on this site, the better it will be for you and could even save your or a friend's life, as realising that you are seeing someone who may have a behaviour problem could be a lifesaver. That is, IF they have been caught or reported.

The important thing here is to deal with this matter quickly and don't say a word to your partner. If the answer comes back positive I would suggest you refrain from any contact as soon as possible, if you know what is good for you, and never allow them any access to your finances.

Non-molestation orders at many family courts are toothless enforcement against narcissistic people, as narcissists are experts at making themselves out to be the victims and getting the judges and Cafcass upon their side.

An injunction is what you need to ask for to deal with

these types of people, as this could mean that the offender is sent to prison if they break the order.

But after speaking to several women who were themselves victims of abuse, who had their cases heard by Basingstoke Family Court district judges, they realised the truth is that the law is protecting the offenders instead of supporting or protecting the victims of abuse, and so they feel ignored and deserted by the British legal system.

Nowadays, it seems that far too many cases that I have read or heard about find the family court district judges are more likely to come down upon the offender's side whilst ignoring the victim's evidence at every opportunity. This seems to often be the case.

This is especially true when cases involve children, as NPD sufferers are very experienced liars and are quite capable of turning everything around in their favour, making their ex-partner out to be the bad person whilst they are the real victims. And the truth here is, the real victims are often ignored by the family court system, judges, Cafcass, and Family Services.

It has now become quite evident in many cases that no matter how much strong evidence and proof of abusive threats is collected by the victim, this evidence is still totally ignored by family court district judges.

One such Basingstoke Family Court district judge seemed to abuse his position by ignoring the rights of victims of abuse to receive a fair hearing, due to his continual bias and support of abusive ex-partners.

I have also been informed that this same district judge has refused to consider evidence from other women on other occasions, who have been unlucky enough for their case to come before him.

I know of a case where the female split with her partner when their child was just over a year old, and after the female informed him that she had enough of his abusive ways, the male turned around and told her that he would **"end her life" or disfigure her so the child would not recognise her.** The male continued to verbally abuse her and added that he would break the legs of each family member so that she had nobody to look after her small child.

Hampshire Police were called to the property where they were living upon the night of this offence and the young woman showed the two male officers a recording of these threats on her mobile phone to prove what she was telling them was the truth.

The police officers promptly did nothing, informing her that she had to leave the property (which belonged to her family), whilst the ex-partner remained there.

Two weeks later, the ex-partner changed all the locks on the property and her father evicted him. I know this case went before this district judge, where he refused to listen to the woman's solicitor, or view/hear a single item of this victim's evidence (both video and text message).

Her evidence of abuse against her ex-partner was massive and so damning that it would have proved without any doubt that he made these threats, along with endless others during their relationship.

But instead, this district judge, who is supposed to be in this position of trust to give a fair and non-biased hearing, refused to listen to a word that this young woman said.

Because of the actions of this narrow-minded district judge in Basingstoke Family Court who seemed to dislike women, she was refused a fair hearing, whilst her ex-partner lied his way through every second of it, but the judge paid attention to everything he said, then turned to this young woman and told her that he refused to accept any of her evidence and dismissed every single item as unacceptable without even looking at a single piece of it. Then this judge went as far as suggesting that she was lying. One-sided or what?

This took place in a Basingstoke Family Court (Hampshire) in 2016 and this same judge continues to sit and hear other cases relating to family breakups and manages to ignore the rights of victims of abuse, simply because they are females and therefore, he is fully against them.

But, still **NOTHING** is done to stop these Miscarriages of Justice.

Even after the victim's father made complaints to the court about this, the judge was allowed to continue to sit upon this young woman's future hearings, where he chastised her at every opportunity. (A fair court system, I do not think so.)

The evidence of this case has been kept in a safe place and is still there, should proof be required.

It does seem to me that the family court supported by Cafcass are protecting the guilty whilst ignoring the victims, which is no surprise to me as this is often the case, nowadays in the British legal system.

It does make you sick, however, when these people sit in judgement, whilst failing to do their duty to uphold the laws that are put in place to protect victims of abuse, simply because their personal views differ from the guidelines. Maybe it is time this old man was forced to retire.

I am also sorry to say that a formal complaint to this same court service only received a reply that these judges are under their own jurisdiction and control and therefore make their own decisions, "so this means that they can ignore the rules to suit their own personal agenda" (letters kept).

There was also a complaint made to those who oversee our court services and even to the PM at the time, which were all referred back to the judge. Anyway, who in their right mind can trust politicians?

What a farce and a total waste of time having a legal system which allows these people who are supposed to uphold the law to do as they please. Those who seem to be beyond the reach of the law book are only answerable to themselves.

This matter was made worse as the lady in question had a child with this individual during their relationship, and this family court judge forced a victim of abuse to remain in contact with her abuser, due to giving them 50/50 custody of their child.

So whilst this is promoted by these judges, these sick individuals are allowed to continue their barrage of abuse upon their ex-partners every single time that they meet to hand the child/children over, which is the case in this matter, simply because nobody wishes to challenge these biased judges.

But this is normally the situation in these cases, as the victims are unable to afford thousands of pounds for a barrister to take their case to High Court or represent them, and so they are crapped upon by the British legal system.

This is truly cause for concern, especially if the partner is a narcissist who has put their ex-partner through hell and done everything in their power to hurt them, both through controlling, emotional abuse and continual threats, because they are allowed by so-called "British Justice" to continue their campaign of hatred, control and threats. They can do nothing to stop this.

So threats can also include failing to make any child support payments or even lying through their arses in court about having no money, then threatening to get full custody and take the child away.

Now at this point, the ex from hell will be using every opportunity to cause as much stress as possible. They feel that they are invincible due to our court system, supported by Cafcass and Family Services, giving them 50/50 custody of their child/children due to short-sighted government guidelines and certain judges who should spend some time behind bars themselves.

I have spoken to many women about this subject and one lady gave me information concerning her daughter's ex-partner and a case that was also heard in Basingstoke Family Court.

Their relationship broke down and her daughter's ex-partner decided to move from the South of England and relocate to the North. This was done totally of his own free will.

This man then applies to the family court who then informed the mother of his child that she will have to travel up to where he has relocated, every two weeks, at her own expense or she will be in breach of their court order.

So you may well understand why at this point the victims may be apprehensive about becoming emotionally involved in the future and will often decide to remain single.

So why does the Basingstoke Family Court along with so many other family courts throughout the UK, and Cafcass, ignore the rights of the **VICTIMS OF ABUSE**, but support abusers against the right of victims. Could it be that

Cafcass employ so many women that can be charmed by these NPD sufferers, due to them turning on the charm at interviews, or just the BS rights of fathers?

Surely, the problem is far deeper than a few judges who are anti-women and should be dismissed.

I do, however, believe that a complete review of the family court system, Cafcass, along with Family Services, is long overdue and any reviews should be carried out by people who know what they are doing and have far greater training to understand Narcissistic Behaviour and Coercive Control.

A few women and some men suggested that lie detectors should be enforced in the court system. Even though they are not foolproof, surely they could put some of those who wish to manipulate the legal system off their game enough for real justice to shine through.

So I ask, surely other judges in the courts will know what is happening, so why have they not spoken out? Or is it such a closed shop and judges are so blinkered in their opinions toward abuse victims that it is nearly impossible to get a fair decision? Or maybe undertaking greater training is needed and for the few to not be involved in abuse cases independently until there is a far greater understanding of Narcissist Controllers in our legal system.

Complete recordings of all cases where abuse has been alleged should also be part of the legal system requirements, so victims can recall that judges refused to listen to evidence, or have shown little or no concern for victims of abuse, or disallow the evidence of abuse victims, so this can be proved and these judges can be removed from our court system.

Until the family courts and Cafcass train their staff to understand Coercive Control and how narcissists manipulate the legal system within this country, nothing will change and they will be guilty of allowing the abuse of victims to continue, and even the death of the victims of these sick people. Also, if a person has assaulted a partner in his past then this should never be removed from their criminal record and should always be used as evidence, as it shows they are capable of violence.

You may not have realised that the person you are with has a screw loose when you first got together, as they are experts at hiding their true self and personality, but the fact is they are not very nice people. You will surely get to know that they are twisted in the head when something goes wrong in your relationship.

Many men and women that I have spoken with have at some time encountered these narcissistic types and regretted it. I know that many of them will bleed you dry financially due to the number of people who have told of events during relationships, and then when they took them to court they lied, turning events around against the victim.

But there are ways to catch them out and there are many books and information out there now and also on the internet.

If you ever come across one of these you must accumulate as much evidence as possible to disprove their lies as they are always bragging about being great parents and financially supporting their child/children when you know that they are not.

Emails, text messages, and video recordings are all great ways to prove what they are like and if you have children, keep the evidence safe till they are old enough to understand.

Narcissists are always at the top of their form when it comes to manipulation, lying and deceit and they will do anything and everything to destroy you and your relationship with your child/children.

This is speaking from experience, but then you cannot guarantee that the judge will listen and this is where instructing a barrister is worth the fees, but who can afford them?

Some of the tactics that narcissists will use are:

1. Narcissistic types will use your child or children as a tool against you both emotionally, financially and in court.

2. Narcissistic types will move as far away as possible so that the other partner has to travel to collect their child or children in the hope that they will give up, or they will try to give you the run-around upon your designated day by leaving a note stuck to the front door saying, "Gone to my mother's," which would be a round journey of 170 miles, back where you travelled from.

3. Another time the excuse will be that your child is unwell, has gone to a party or has slept over at a friend's home 85 miles away, back to where you travelled from.

4. Narcissistic types will not let you take your child/children away on holiday then they take the child/children to Spain or further with their latest boyfriend/girlfriend.

5. Narcissistic types will damage your vehicle to make it as hard as possible for you to travel to pick up your child/children.

6. If the narcissist is from another country then be prepared for their threats to take the child to see their family, as there is a very good chance you will have to fight to get the child/children back again.

7. Promotes themselves to other parents at their school as a top caring person, then dresses the child in hand-me-down clothes that his girlfriend's children wore previously.

This list can be endless.

A delusional Coercive Controller will use all types of dirty tricks and many men and women and their new partners have suffered endless embarrassment or harassment over the years.

This behaviour is not reserved to men only.

A man stated to me that his memory of a narcissistic controlling relationship was after he broke up with this person. Both she and her father stalked him for weeks, just so they could check where he was going and who he was seeing.

There was a fire escape which went up to a glass door at the rear of his flat in Berkshire, which was used to enter and leave the property. This was where they stood to spy upon him through the glass door and even intercepted his mail on a few occasions.

They made his life a living misery, including damaging his property or making abusive calls and then hanging up in the early hours of the morning.

The hatred they hold can be quite scary. So watch it out there, guys and girls.

Please remember that not all fathers/mothers give a damn about their children and so this section is aimed as a warning to the few who care and are troubled by real-life Coercive Controllers who will go out of their way to destroy everything in your life to get their way.

This is one of the reasons it is so hard to understand the line of thought that some ex-partners take when they are jilted; they seem to go into destruction mode with a desire to do you harm, or any other person who dares to even look at you.

Remember that Coercive Controlling types do not look any different from others, but they are quite capable of going to any lengths to cause you trouble and stop you from seeing your child/children.

Coercive Controllers are so sure of themselves that they cannot tell the difference between lies and the truth, so in the end, it is quite easy to catch them off guard, if you are smart enough.

A controlling person will clear out your bank account and rob you blind if they get the chance, taking your house and everything else they can get their hands on, leaving you with the clothes you wear.

If your child has the misfortune to live with this person for any period then you can guarantee that they could finish up as a carbon copy of their mother or father, whoever is the controlling ex-partner, with a strong desire to sexually rob their future partners of everything if they cannot get their way.

There is a saying "better to be safe than sorry" and speaking from real-life experience, I recommend that any man/woman who owns their property must safeguard themselves.

An appointment with a solicitor for a financial agreement is an extremely sound investment, which was not available when I needed one. But any agreement must be arranged and signed before the person moves in otherwise there is a damn good chance of you losing everything if anything goes wrong, especially if there is a child or children involved as Psycho types will stop at nothing.

I was told of one person who tried to get his girlfriend's parents to sell their property so they could hand over the proceeds to him and he could invest in properties for their future in another country. Apparently, the father said to their wife that this person was out of his mind if he thought they trusted him enough to give him a penny.

Always remember that if they refuse to sign any legal document that will safeguard your financial well-being, then you can be sure that they cannot be trusted or are out for their own financial well-being, and DO NOT believe anything they say to try to change your mind about this agreement.

If you have a child/children with them then the first rule to remember is to make sure that no support payments or any cash are ever handed over, and I mean ANY, without obtaining a receipt, as they always deny in court that you have paid anything, and will argue that you have never supported your child or her financially in any way since the child was born.

Another good idea is a blood test to prove parenthood.

Remember, hundreds of thousands of pounds go to ex-partners each year and many good fathers and mothers are shafted by the courts for non-payment of maintenance, when they have paid up to date and therefore do not deserve it.

A lot of ex-partners stand up in front of a judge with crocodile tears in their eyes and tell endless lies, as their main goal is to make you look like a total waste of space.

Some judges seem to show their dislike towards women who are the victims in many of these cases. Just where is the justice?

Many partners will try to hit their ex-partner where it hurts (in the pocket), normally supported by divorced or separated friends or family members and of course, the Child Support Agency and Cafcass (just two of society's bloodsuckers).

The CSA seems to believe that the person who is bringing up a child can live upon ten pounds a week, whilst they hand most of their wages over to the ex from hell, who normally has another partner on the go, and tells the courts that they are finding it impossible to survive on the cash they get from you. Many departments refuse to chase the ex-partner as they take their word when told that they earn very little.

I have spoken to lots of successful businessmen and women who honestly believe that many of the ex-partners that they have come into contact with seem to be more aware of the financial benefits obtainable through relationships with offspring nowadays, and are upon the prowl for that certain person with the nice car and their own house. This is one of the reasons a financial agreement is strongly advised and supported these days, if you wish to keep your property and bank balance.

Well, the odd night stay-over may be OK, but be aware that this can soon turn into a moving-in event or maybe an accidental pregnancy that just happened at the wrong moment, if no agreement has been signed.

An unplanned pregnancy can damn any financially stable person and create distrust between the couple if one of you didn't want it.

Another reason is that you have not known each other for any period, or if the person who moves in is not in a similar financial position as yourself. This is also a possible stumbling block.

Trust is a strong bond and you must be able to trust the other person, but you must safeguard yourself, After all, you can't be sure if they wanted to be with you for your money. I am fully aware that this is not a nice way to view people, but better to be safe than sorry, as it does happen.

I would like to point out that women must also take on board the facts about owning property, as there are quite a few men who are just as capable of cleaning out your bank account and leaving you high and dry. The possibilities are endless where money is concerned.

Trust with time; don't jump into things or you may be sorry.

I know that you may be sitting there reading this and thinking, *Is he serious?* I am deadly serious, as I can assure you that losing hundreds or thousands of pounds is not an easy thing to suffer.

By this time it may be a good idea to emphasise that not all ex-partners are like this, as some are excellent and close friends, going beyond the realms to support their ex-partner where their child or children are concerned.

But, anyone who has ever come across a Controller can tell you that it will never be an enjoyable experience and the bad memories of this meeting will remain with you and haunt you for years to come. Sometimes it can be nearly impossible to settle into another relationship in the future due to their behaviour.

Some ex-partners refuse to support their children financially. They will do everything to demand their rights to the child/children, whilst they plead poverty to the court and have a business on the side and also work for another company at the same time, which the British court system does not wish to know.

Whilst all this is going on they continue to buy apartments overseas to build up their future, whilst having a view of stealing the child away and then moving to another country. I know this sounds bad, but it happens and our court system allows it by ignoring the abused partners.

Then again, NOT all Controllers tell their partners the real truth about their past, like assaults on previous partners, and even why their relationships do not last more than one year. But I am sure you will soon find out if you get involved with one.

The only good news is, in the past few years there has been a change in the law and the introduction of Coercive Control law, which makes this a criminal offence, has been introduced into law, but how can it help when the courts, Cafcass and the system ignore the rights of Victims of Abuse?

It may, however, take some time for intelligence to arrive in Parliament and bring about solid enforcement to protect the innocent and remove judges who are untrained or anti-victim. Forcing some judges to abide by set rules, instead of thinking up their own, would also be a good move in our Family Court system.

Or shall we ask, "How many more innocent victims' lives will be taken before those in government do what is right?"

Far too many victims are being ignored, whilst their mentally sick partners/ex-partners put them and their offspring through Hell.

This controlling behaviour is designed to make a person dependent by isolating them from support, exploiting them, depriving them of independence and regulating their everyday behaviour so they thus become submissive.

The main thing that I have found out concerning those who control and threaten their partners, is that their fathers were cowards like them who treated their wives the same way, but the problem is that these people will continue until they kill someone.

Thanks to Women's Aid, which has endlessly campaigned and succeeded in achieving this change in the law.

Let's hope that the police and courts get their act together to support this law fully, soon.

Domestic abuse of someone isn't always physical.

Coercive control is an act or a pattern of acts of assault, threats, humiliation and intimidation or other abuse that is used to harm, punish, or frighten the victim.

DO NOT ALLOW THIS TO CONTINUE.

Some interesting parts taken from Court Bench Book 3.

Introduction: The Equal Treatment and the Judge Equal Treatment Bench Book 3 Introduction: Equal Treatment and the Judge Introduction.

I will do right to all manner of people after the laws and usages of this realm, without fear or favour, affection or ill will.

1. Fair treatment is a fundamental principle embedded in the judicial oath and is, therefore, a vital judicial responsibility. For many judges, this will be how they will approach much of the guidance provided in this bench book. For most, the principles of fair treatment and equality will be inherent in everything they do as

judges and they will understand the concepts very well. The Bench Book seeks to support and build on that understanding. It is not intended to be prescriptive, but simply to inform, assist and guide.

2. Although the Bench Book does not express the law, judges are encouraged to take its guidance into account wherever applicable.

3. To ensure equality before the law, a judge must be free from prejudice and partiality and conduct themselves, in and out of court, to give no ground for doubting their ability and willingness to decide cases solely on their legal and factual merit.

This should give many victims of abuse the knowledge that far too many judges within the family court are prejudiced and failing in their duties.

Under the title of Domestic Violence and Abuse Domestic Violence 36

The government defines domestic violence as any incident of threatening behaviour, violence or abuse (psychological, physical, sexual, financial or emotional) between adults who are or have been intimate partners or family members, regardless of gender or sexuality. Including so-called 'honour-based violence'.

37. On average two women in England and Wales are killed every week by current or former male partners.

38. Fewer than 1 in 4 who suffer abuse at the hands of their partner- and 1 in 10 women who experience serious sexual assault- report it to the police.

This does make me ask the question – WHY do they not report it? Maybe it could have something to do with the current police and courts' lack of support, or the view that they will not be believed or accused of lying, especially.

If you have ever been a victim of abuse, did you feel supported by the police and court system?

Of course, there will always be those in society who seem to be born with this gene built in and most of these look upon their life as it is their right to mistreat their partners and use them as servants or simply a punchbag, till they come across someone who will stand up to them and return the favour.

A man who beat a woman is a coward.

A woman that kicked a man's arse after he beat her

IS A HERO.

Remember, a woman is many things, but stupid is not generally one of them, and as a woman is capable of knowing what a man is like within seconds of him opening his mouth upon their first meeting, surely the best thing to do is keep quiet, smile and let the lady do all the talking.

Unfortunately, so many of us guys are just incapable of doing this, as we try to impress the ladies straight away with endless chat and so whilst we men are fumbling around in their underpants, most women would have looked us up and down and made a clear decisive decision as to the type of person we are. Wonderful or wimp, lover or liar, it is up to you what her choice will be. Remember to engage your brain before opening your mouth.

But, one of the greatest worries to any "sensible" male nowadays is if you should be approached a young woman in a bar or nightclub, how can you be sure if this woman is even old enough to be there? And you can never really guarantee that a female will tell you the truth concerning her age. It is not, however, a good thing to start your conversation by saying, "Hi, I'm Tom, how old are you?" or, "Can I see your birth certificate?"

Whilst some girls look eighteen-plus, in reality, their real age can be as young as fourteen or even younger, as they dress to make themselves look much older to get into clubs and bars.

You would hope that if they are in a public house, then they are of the lawful age to be there, but that is not anywhere near the truth and many men have found out that the result can end up with them in prison.

If you are a parent you will be fully aware of just how good our teenage offspring are at telling us "Porkies", so can we trust what they tell us when they go out with their friends? Sorry, but most of the time we cannot, you just have to trust them and hope.

So many young people are sexually aware and active nowadays and thanks to the world around us it seems as if everyone is promoting sex to sell everything.

Parents have to deal with a lot of stress and worry when they have children. The younger children it is the endless bad moods and paddy throwing, and then when they get older it is the lack of interest in listening to their parents. The worries are endless especially if they have girls.

Being a father, you only have to think back to your teens and you realise that most boys of their age are walking hormones.

The problem is that a daughter can bring home many worries, as growing up in today's society often means that young women are pushed into losing their virginity or sleeping around by other girls whilst in their early teens so they can be accepted into the girl group, and the fact that most teenage boys target girls whom they know to be virgins so they can brag to their friends. It seems to be all about showing off to your mates. Teenage life can be an endless fight for fashion and fitting into the "Popular Groups".

When you have a family the worry of having teenagers can

create many arguments between the parents and other family members. Anyway, there are a lot of sick-minded people in this world who would view young girls dressed up as easy bait.

Being a good parent means worrying about your children and this will not end even when they reach adulthood. This is where learning to communicate with your offspring can assist you both in working together to improve and build upon your skills as a partnership, even though most of the time your offspring will not listen to you.

Showing your children that you understand will guide them as they grow up to hopefully confide in you, thus being able to communicate with you both, but do not allow them to play one of you against the other or to manipulate a situation to their advantage as this is always a popular trick that they are experts at from a very young age.

We often look at our children as innocent youngsters, even when they are in their late teens. But the main concern is that we were all that age at one time and so are fully aware of what goes on, but until we grow up and realise that trust is a good base for living by, our life will never be a smooth journey.

There is only one problem when dealing with your offspring and that is whether you can be 100% sure that they are telling you the whole story or the truth. This is why gaining their trust and being able to talk openly with them is so important.

Teenagers are and always will be a Pain in the Butt; you more than likely were and they are doing the same to you.

Now, we all understand why so many parents have health problems whilst dealing with their offspring growing up.

Now you realise what your parents went through when you were growing up. Payback is a bitch, don't you think?

Don't worry, it will be the same for them when they have children of their own and when they come running to you for advice, it will be your time to say, "Now you understand what your mother and I went through, and by the way, the Bank of Mum and Dad has shut its doors."

It is amazing how many people mentioned that they had a daughter who had a child with an ex-partner even though she was warned by her parents not to get pregnant, as they were always having arguments and her parents felt that she was too immature and he was an unstable person who often went into a rage over the smallest matter, also often abusive to the girl and her mother.

The daughter split up with the boyfriend as he was an A-hole (as it was put).

It seems that the natural course was that the girl got a place with the child, whilst she still expected her parents to stop their life and give their time to looking after her child, whilst she continued to live her life as she wished.

Her parents were used as private babysitters and spent hours with their grandchild, whom they loved, but failed to receive any thanks for their time from their daughter. The only expectation from her was that they would continue to assist her both financially and with babysitting.

Then after living on her own she got into massive debt and moved back to her parents who continued to be the financial bank until their savings were exhausted, whilst she continued to spend, spend, spend and expected her parents to still maintain their support.

Does This Ring A Note?

Amazingly, throughout the child's life, the waster father continued to plead poverty so that he did not have to pay maintenance and gave second-hand clothes to the child when he had her. Even though he gained 50/50 custody he continued to create as many problems as he could for the mother of the child. This can also happen in reverse.

Surely a stronger investigation into these lame parents who lie to hide their finances so they can remove themselves from any financial responsibility to their offspring is long overdue.

They manage to live a good life, whilst their ex-partners struggle to feed and cloth their child. This is wrong and the law needs to be changed so that a father or mother cannot refuse to support their child financially, no matter what.

We all find relationships to be a real hard task at some point or another. The main problem in most relationships is couples. Yes, I mean it, "couples". It's all in that word. When you become a "couple" you become a partnership and this is where so many of us go wrong, as we try to carry on as if we were still "single".

Having a real bond with your partner sometimes sneaks up on you when you don't expect it and you spend any time away from them wishing you were with them, thinking about laying there in each other's arms, laughing about nothing really, but enjoying every second together.

This changes as soon as you become a unit together. This means that you take a certain responsibility towards the other person as it is no longer suitable to continue taking the same old day-to-day actions as you did when you were single.

But it is hard to be doing your own thing for so long and all of a sudden there is another person in your life whom you have emotions for, meaning that your life takes a completely new direction.

Being truthful is very important when you decide to start this partnership; it means that it is time for you to grow up and put away all the childish stupidity in your life. Yes, it is all right to laugh, but a different type of laugh, the type that removes those silly risks and chances of being a single person.

4. Right or Wrong

When you were single and out with your mates, life was less responsible, but now your life unit involves another human being, another person to hurt, if you go wrong.

This does not mean that your life must end. It does, however, mean that taking a serious look at yourself and your partner and then working together as a grown-up pair of adults and not playing like children anymore. It means being able to talk with each other about problems and concerns, not throwing a paddy because you cannot have everything "your own way".

Consider this: why do so many "couples" fail when they move in together? Simple. Neither of them take into account that their lives will be different as it will no longer be "My Space" – it becomes "Our Space" and you both must remember the four rules of partnership: "Share", "Care", "Trust", and "Consideration".

Learn to talk openly about problems or concerns each day like money worries or the fact that one of you works, whilst the other is sat at home all day. The problem is that the longer you leave a problem, the harder it becomes to talk about. Remember, a problem can kill off any partnership.

The hardest thing for a partner to cope with in any relationship is being put down, or the feeling you get when you come up with what you consider to be a great idea, only to have your partner extinguish your enthusiasm in a split second. This is twice as bad if done in front of friends.

A condescending attitude from a partner is something that is never acceptable. It is hard to accept a remark when it seems intended to humiliate or criticise you in front of friends, and this can feel like the person you are with holds less respect or care towards you than originally thought.

Being inconsiderate to a partner, especially when you are in a long-term relationship, can cause endless damage to that relationship and start far too many arguments, so best think before you speak.

Being with the same person for a long time can often be stressful and boring, though this does differ in each relationship. You sometimes find banter that is used as harmless fun depending upon the strength of your relationship, and if the banter becomes detrimental remarks in front of a certain male or female friend every time you are out with them, then the partner needs to address that matter sooner rather than later, as there may be some possible underlying attraction.

However, in many relationships, there are often arguments over stupid things and these arguments can get quite heated, but in most relationships, they fizzle out as quickly as they started.

Sometimes heated exchanges can take place with seemingly odd reactions, such as one minute you can be thinking, *Bitch*, or, *Bastard*, but a couple of minutes later looking into their eyes, thinking, *I could do nice things to you*. This goes to show that in the male's case our little man (penis) does a lot of our thinking for us as usual, and this is one of the reasons why women have us blokes by the balls. They do like to show their man who's in charge and use moments such as these to their advantage.

There will also be times when you think to yourself, *Should I walk away and call it a day?* as you feel that your life is going nowhere. This can be made worse if one of you seems lazy to the other or fails to earn anything, thus creating a bad feeling that one of you is doing all the paying, but this situation can be different if you have an arrangement due to offspring or health problems.

Remember, if it has got to the stage where you can't stand each other and are unable to speak, then maybe it is simply the end of the road in this relationship and sometimes it is far easier to end it than both of you living a life of hell with someone who you seem to hate more each day.

I also found that both sexes can be extremely condescending towards the opposite sex in both a playful and serious way, but this does not achieve anything and can cause friction between them, and there is a simple way around this condescending behaviour. "Chat." Yes, maintaining the ability to carry out a proper adult conversation with a person of the opposite sex over anything will often assist you with the rest. Talking about concerns and problems is a great way to build strength within a relationship, thus creating a stronger bond between you whilst improving trust in each other. Always remember that trust is a strong glue in any relationship, and laughter is also a good mix to help you grow stronger together. Anyway, who wants to be in a relationship where there is argument after argument and both of you have a face as long as a wet weekend?

Another thing is being able to say sorry to each other after a disagreement. I think that you should never go to bed angry, as it becomes a lot harder facing each other the next morning and even harder to apologise to a woman who still has her angry head on. "Yes," I did say that we apologise, as that is how it normally works when a man disagrees with a woman.

Anyway, sometimes making up is such good fun as well and when in a long-term relationship, sorry, but it is an easier word to say.

Relationships can be very hard work at the best of times as some males and females are useless at maintaining relationships for any period of time. They find it easier to have female or male friends without emotional ties, just simple sex. I am sure that having friendships like this can be amazingly less stressful than the involvement of a full-on relationship and in many ways, this can bring a certain harmony into your life.

But what happens if you should cross the line and allow emotions to become involved? Well then the situation can soon be turned upside down, often spoiling a very good friendship, which may never be the same again. I know that a few of us have been in this situation which is often called the practice of "shooting yourself in the foot". A guy told me of a member of his family many years ago, after he mentioned how he felt about a female friend they let it slip in front of the person, making him feel like a total idiot. If you spend time with a person you should be able to get signs through their body language to give you some idea, but do not rush into anything as it could backfire.

Being in a relationship is not always a smooth ride and both men and women know that a great deal of their time with their partner in any relationship will be spent trying to keep them happy and content. 'As long as they are happy, so are we.' However, men tend to get sloppy and give up trying after some time and accept their fate (settling into a routine/rut). This is how we go wrong. If you stimulate a relationship you will help to improve it and this can be a bonus both in and out of the bedroom as well as in your day-to-day life. The bedroom is not the only place to engage in your fantasies with your partner if they are like-minded or game for a "bit of fun" or like to whisper sexy words in each other's ears.

During the early stages of any relationship, the emotional

and sexual excitement can at times push you to the very edge of mental exhaustion; it seems that you can become obsessed with the belief that you have found your perfect partner, thinking that you will live in harmony forever. This is of course a total fantasy, as you may be happy in the early stages, but the problem that everyone has to deal with when deciding to settle with a partner is that finding the right one is not always instant.

It feels that the other person is everything that you have ever wanted, but give it some time together and a few arguments and you may feel a whole lot differently towards them, but they always say, "True love never runs smoothly," so it could be true love and only time will tell.

However, this will never last if you do not try to understand the person that you are with, as a woman's mood can change over the slightest thing and these mood swings can last for hours or days, so trying a little harder, you guys can soften the blow.

Many of us males do tend to screw up relationships and it is as if we were born with the ability to cause ourselves problems by allowing our manhood to overrule any sensible line of thought.

This is an action often referred to by women as, "Men thinking with our dicks," and many of us men are fully aware that we could have done without the help of our penis's guidance upon many occasions. The ladies are certainly 100% right there.

So what makes women do the wrong thing and become involved with the wrong man? Poor judgement or just an off day, or maybe the guy was just a charmer?

We all know that we humans put on a front when we first meet a member of the opposite sex, should we be attracted to them.

Whilst, if it is at all possible for a man to change his direction of thought away from his "little mate" (penis), then there may be a slight possibility that common sense may prevail, and you never know, you could even finish up in a reasonable and mostly happy relationship, but I think most men understand that as soon as our penis starts getting involved, we are screwed as common sense just goes out the window.

But men are so often misled by beautiful women with breasts on display and legs that seem to go up and up, whilst our temperatures do the same. Well, who in their right mind can blame a man for losing his way?

I must point out that not all the fault is the man's, as we all understand that living with a woman can quite often be extremely stressful, and at times some women will use their equipment to purposely mislead us poor misguided men from the straight and narrow.

Yes, we men do go wrong and become distracted by other flashes of flesh, such as cleavage. Yes, come on, boys, wake up and get your brains out of your underpants, but what can you expect when it is all on show?

But why do partners stray and play around with other men and women? Could it be boredom as their sex life has just run out of juice, or is it the excitement of being caught by their partners? Maybe it is just being a horny bastard. Whichever way you look at it, you have just fucked up your marriage and it does not matter even if you both tried to rebuild it, even if you are never caught, the guilt will get you in the end. Your relationship will never be the same again and if you have a family, they will be the ones who suffer, children included.

There is also fallout damage to take into account; this is where you both employ solicitors to handle your divorce and whilst you guys are bitching, moaning and doing whatever you can to screw your partner out of every penny you can, those greedy, bloodsucking legal representatives will be rubbing their hands together and watching their invoices getting larger and larger.

Now think back to why you split and whose fault it was that it happened.

The answer is plain and simple: both of you allowed your relationship to become so stale and this was why there was no spark left, therefore both of you had given up caring.

This is normal when couples drift apart and you both feel that there is nothing there to stay together for anymore.

This is where you are wrong. This is why both males and females are vulnerable at this time and you can be sure that there will always be some slug, whether it be male or female, who will take this opportunity to make their move.

Now, if you had both taken the time to sit and talk about how you were feeling earlier and what concerns you both, then your life would not be upon the rim of the toilet at present, awaiting your legal representatives to pull the flush, as their only concern is how much they will be earning out of ending your marriage. It seems that so many divorces legals are money motivated.

Relationships need to be a two-way street, but it seems that the main problems in any relationship are disagreements.

Especially if it gets to a stage when a woman will not admit when she is at fault, and a man will not admit when he is at fault, a continual circle where disagreement after disagreement is never resolved, normally ending after a few hours with neither having the slightest idea what the argument was about in the first place, but still blaming each other for being the instigator.

Many such arguments can start for the simplest of reasons and this can show a man the errors of his ways in arguing with a woman, as he finds he will never win.

Remember that a woman has a way of recalling events and disagreements long after they have passed, even though she may not always remember them in their original context. She can remember for a lot longer than we males can and any argument can be reignited by the slightest word out of place in the future and brought back to be used against you in the hours, days, weeks, months, maybe years to come.

Truth is that we men are screwed at this point, simply because men argue and then forget it most of the time, whilst a woman does not forget as easily and can hold a grudge, so be warned. Treat them nice, and keep them loving.

Another problem that we males have is the fact that men tend to laugh things off when they cannot think of a sensible answer or when a woman confronts them over something, but if she asks a simple question, expecting a straightforward answer, then she is expecting just that, a straightforward answer, and you had better give it to her.

Be very careful as a woman can soon become extremely irate if she thinks that you are laughing at her, and a man's biggest mistake is to show signs of a condescending attitude toward a woman because if he does not answer right and this turns into an argument, she will move you to the doghouse for a very long time.

So try some sensible replies for a change. "Think before you speak."

Most of the time, if both of you had taken the time to simply chat about problems earlier, then just maybe you would not have come this far.

During any relationship, being open and speaking to each other about concerns helps you to clear matters up before they get too out of control.

Yes, there have been many books written by "experts" stating that science has proved this and that, and information they have formulated shows that because a woman and man answer questions in a certain way this proves that they would be attracted to each other, or are in some way compatible. What a total load of bullshit. Whilst expert (?) knowledge may be a good thing in certain areas, it can never be replaced by good old common sense and interaction with these adorable mind-blowing creatures. This is the same as children experts who have never had a child, as you don't know until you do it.

You can ask most men a question about their feelings for women and get a semi-sensible reply around 50% of the time, but when it comes to why he is attracted to a woman, he may stand there with that vacant look on his face for some time before he will reply, "I don't know."

Nowadays the answer is as simple as this, SEX, because she has a nice figure and he feels that he stands a chance to get her into bed. He will try anything to get her attention, even going as far as running himself around like a fool trying to impress, whilst she allows him to make a fool of himself just to see how far he will go for her. All this and she does not have to be the greatest beauty in the place (though this sometimes helps).

However, this changes for every person, as the saying goes: "beauty is in the eye of the beholder." Then again, the level of beauty can also be multiplied depending upon the amount of alcohol that has been consumed during that day or night, as I am sure both males and females can relate to going to bed with the beauty and waking up with a beast. Whilst for some people it does not matter, as it simply comes down to "because they have a pulse".

Many women made comments that what impresses them when meeting a guy is often the way he dresses. Also some women will fancy him depending on the amount of cash he is spending. It can also be down to the effort that he puts into his introduction when he first approaches her.

Another time, it can be as pure and simple as she fancies having sex with someone. It is not always the male, who is out on the pull. Besides, it does not mean that they will be a compatible couple; on most occasions, it does show the animal instinct in human nature and that sex has entered the equation.

Whilst upon the subject of "bumps", I had a good friend many years ago who used to put a rolled-up pair of socks down the front of his underpants when going nightclubbing as he said it helped him pick up women, and it seem to work as he always scored, until one night he was wearing loose-fitting boxer short and the socks fell out upon the floor, whilst he was dancing. I have never laughed so much since that time.

Most people will understand that in our modern-day society sex plays a large part in everyday life, along with all attractions, as it has done in every mating ritual involving a man and a woman since the first cave-man clubbed a woman. But with these days being times of equal opportunities, it could be the woman doing the clubbing.

(Those who don't understand, the word "clubbing" refers to a wooden item used hit people on the head.)

Sex should never be the sole basis of any relationship or taken too lightly, even though it is an important part of the emotional side of any relationship. I fully agree that it is also an extremely enjoyable and pleasurable pastime, but it is unwise if it should be cold-heartedly carried out.

If you should decide to build a relationship solely on sex you can guarantee that it will fail sooner rather than later. Do not take this the wrong way, as sex is great and can be fantastic when shared with the right person. (There are some of you who are still willing to remain virgins and save yourselves for that special person to come along. Good luck to you, but remember that there are those out in the world who love virgins and will do almost anything to take that away from you.)

The problem is, it seems that everyone in day-to-day life is using sex to promote anything and everything, and so you can understand why people have such a liberal approach towards sex when it is used to sell or promote products in this manner and is part of everyday life.

Quote from Paul at a stag night:

If you happen to meet a woman in a bar or nightclub and on the first night she gives you a blowjob, I would strongly suggest that this is not a sound foundation for a long-term relationship.

Try to remember this.

Of course, there are and always will be those people who will use sex as a simple manipulation tool to get what they want, and it does not always mean that you will be rewarded with sex afterwards. It could simply be a "Come On" to get you to buy drinks or spend your money upon them (this is called Dangling the Carrot).

Those money-grabbing types are the worst ones to become involved with, as they will normally destroy you given the chance should you upset them in some way or another. If you happen to come across one of these types then I would suggest that you get the word out to your mates concerning their low moral standards.

The easy way to catch them out is to buy them a drink, then when finished say, "It's your round."

Men tend to have little or no comprehension as to why women often get the upper hand over us.

The reason is often quite simple: some men jump into situations without thinking. You need to take a step back and look at their options. Ask some of their male mates what attracts them to a woman and in most cases, the answer that mates give will involve part of the female body used in a sexual act. Try looking at a member of the opposite sex without thinking of sex in some form or another.

Women can try this out as well (as normal, the boys are thinking with the penises again), but the real answer is as simple as "get to know someone by talking to them", as you may find that you have met your soul mate.

Another thing that surprised me was the number of people in relationships who say that they do not look at members of the opposite sex when they are with their partners. This is a total lie as it is human nature to window shop, but it does not mean that you have to go in and try something on, if you get my meaning.

You can be very happy with a partner, both satisfied in the direction that your relationship is going, but never take them for granted as there is always a chance, no matter how slight, that somewhere down the road they may meet someone who catches their eye or with whom they feel an attraction, and unless you keep that same strong, loving, emotional connection with each other as you had in the peak of your relationship, you could lose them, especially if you spend a lot of your time together arguing. Also, the longer that you are together, the harder it becomes to keep the happiness in a relationship.

Often sex with the same partner can become repetitive and stagnant, leading to one or both partners becoming bored and looking elsewhere.

Relationships are and always will be a two-way street, therefore you must learn to give and take in any relationship otherwise you will destroy any chances of staying together. If you love your partner then make a point of showing them, don't take them for granted, and I can assure you that we have all done this during a relationship. "You do not know what you had till you've lost it."

Men and women need to understand themselves first, as being fully aware of their actions and behaviour can assist them when meeting members of the opposite sex. Honesty, politeness, good humour and being yourself can help you along the way, and the ability to complete a sentence without the word "fuck" can also be a great help. There is nothing worse than a woman who sounds like she has just stepped off a building site or a guy whose sentences mainly consist of the 'F' word, thus making him look like a total moron.

Gaining the ability to observe the body language of others at an early stage is also an advantage, whilst being aware of over-emotional people can also be of help when meeting or becoming involved with members of the opposite sex, as signs of early emotions can be a warning of a relationship minefield. Those who fall in love instantly can often suffer jealousy and be very clingy; try to steer clear unless you like headaches.

Many relationships can be scuttled in the early stages as far too much emphasis is placed upon listening to the views of friends and others instead of working together as a partnership to make your relationship succeed.

Sexual attraction seems to be one of the greatest problem makers known to men or women in modern life. It can happen at any time depending upon your mood and even the clothes you wear. With a man it seems to be a regular daily occurrence due to the amount of legs and cleavage that are on show. How are you supposed to keep your mind off sex when it is in front of you every single time you leave the house? Am I getting old or are women being more provocative these days?

Hemlines seem to shrink further each year, depending upon the fashions, then along came lower cut tops and the amount of cloth used to construct each top and skirt, meaning that there is not only a lot of breast on show, but stomach and knickers too. Also the shorts that some women wear keep very little concealed. Am I being a prude or has self-respect gone out of the window?

Whilst talking to 11 guys at a stag night in the Carpenter's Arms Public House in Camberley, Surrey, I asked the question about the way women dress to get noticed and most of the comments I got back were along the lines of showing everything off, and then the conversation moved to plastic surgery/Botox.

A few guys said they thought that "Getting a Fat Lip" meant receiving a punch in the mouth and not a pair of Fish Lips, which seems to be the fashion nowadays. One guy even stated that he wondered if these women ever became stuck when kissing someone (I expect that would be a vacuum kiss).

Many of their views concerning women and Botox/plastic surgery were strongly felt and every single one agreed that if done tastefully it can be attractive, but so many who have taken the plunge have gone too far and now resemble mannequins rather than beautiful women. They would much prefer natural beauty than plastic dummies who have problems smiling or those monstrous tits that look like she will fall over any second and are so embarrassingly abnormal. I confirmed to them that they understood that not all big-chested women have false tits... These are the 'love myself' type.

I am informed by my daughter and wife that many modern-day women dress as a source of pleasure/self-satisfaction or for the "look good, feel good factor", but my question is this: has self-pleasure taken over or has it just become some sort of game to get the men staring at them, whilst trying to make their partners jealous? Women I have asked did not wish to comment. I call it dressing up like a dog's dinner.

Some relationship experts state that wearing different colours is a way to show your mood.

Colour Psychology by David Johnson.

http://www.infoplease.com/spot/colors1.html *describes how different colours relate to different emotions.*

When going out on the town many people tend to dress in clothes that they feel comfortable in; a pair of jeans, a shirt/jumper, a jacket or maybe a suit, it all depends upon your taste or how you view the way that you like to present yourself.

The thing that men can never understand is how some women can think that they look sexy in clothes such as leggings when they are not built for them, such as having a large stomach hanging over the waistband or protruding out from under a crop-top or blouse. Also those see-through leggings that show off a pair of large granny-type knickers underneath are another turn-off, but even worse than that is a G-string upon some people. Of course, this can relate to men as well as women.

But, this does not mean that males or females need to belittle someone due to the way they are dressed. After all, you do not know their circumstances.

A lot of women that I have spoken to commented about the guy who is unshaven with a large beer belly wearing a stain-covered football shirt that fails to tuck fully into his trousers, but this also shows just how judgemental people in present-day society are nowadays.

Many comments were made stating, "How can he expect to attract the interest of a member of the opposite sex looking like this?"

But it all comes down to the fact that everyone has different levels of taste and some people look at a person and see that they have a nice personality, whilst there will always be those who chat up basically anyone, and solely to get sex at the end of the night.

When asked the question concerning the way people dress, many people have commented that they feel it is better to take some pride in your appearance, clean up your act, maybe lose a little weight, and try wearing clothes which are not so tight or see-through. The idea is to look good to others and not like you have just left a football match.

Many groups made comments like, "Surely better presentation will give you a far greater chance of meeting someone special, but then again there are still many skinny and beautiful people who think that they look good, whilst looking 'yuk'."

One comment was made by a group of girls concerning pride in one's appearance, stating that it is a wonderful thing if you are out on the town with your mates or just out with a friend. There is a far greater chance of admiring someone who is well presented and dressed fashionably in clean clothes with clean hair rather than someone who looks like they have just stolen the clothes from a charity bin at the rear of the local supermarket.

These comments were made by seven young women who were aged between seventeen to nineteen (guess), dressed and looked more like hookers with everything hanging out. I could tell that these girls thought they were really fine, but when I moved on to speak with a group of guys a few tables away, I am sure that the girls would not have appreciated the guys' comments as it seemed that they all came to the same assessment that those girls would be "easy".

When I asked these same men about how they dress to go out the answers were quite consistent, as most thought that a pair of jeans and a top were their normal choice, that is until the wife or girlfriend got involved as at this moment their choice of clothes was replaced by what attire their partner suggested and they did not dare to disagree (happy life).

Pride in your appearance is a thing that comes so easily to many people and by simply looking at those around you, it is possible to get some guidance on how to present yourself and how not to present yourself. It does not matter if you are short of cash as there are plenty of people who are in the same position and still find ways to dress nicely. There are an abundance of charity shops where you can find nice outfits at rock-bottom prices, as well as many main town centre shops that charge very affordable prices, sometimes even better-reduced items. You know who I mean.

A few women mentioned that not all people wish to look like those skinny bone-bag supermodels. Surely, looking like you need a good meal is not normal and who's to say that fashion designers really know what they are doing or talking about? Whilst many men stated that women still look better with curves and bumps in all the right places and without plastic.

The hardest plight that a husband or boyfriend may have is keeping their partner within the boundaries of a reasonable level of happiness, thus allowing a man a certain level of peace.

The one thing that I have found whilst researching this book is just how many men have made the same statements and seem to think the same.

When they first met their partner things seemed to be great, sex was great, she did not object to you having the odd evening out with your mates, and she told you that she would not change a thing about you, even going as far as making a point of telling you that you were her soul mate.

Then came the wedding day and a great time was had by all and everything seemed to be perfect, but wait, a short time later and things start to change, the cracks start to appear. The evenings with your mates is the first thing she demands goes. Then she tells you that she does not like how you dress, or your hair and, "Oh," that beard can go, the beard that she loved so much a short time ago. You end up thinking to yourself, *Where did I go wrong and where in the hell did that hot little girlfriend of mine go?*

Answer: you married her.

These previous comments were made when their wives were not within hearing range, of course.

Many men pointed out that it feels like nothing men do or say will ever be satisfactory and you get the endless feeling that you are in a downward spiral.

Relationships are hard to understand and keep stimulated, whilst marriage often seems to be a licence for some women to turn a man's life into that of a dog, and as soon as we say those magic words, 'I do', this is when the dog gets promoted to a level above that of the husband, and even the dog looks at you with sympathy and disbelief. But you can be assured that many women have suffered from similar punishment.

OK, this is where I have to take a step back and say that not all marriages are such dark places, but no marriage is easy. Some married couples live together with a certain level of happiness for years, but a few guys added, yeah, as long as the man has a garden shed or garage that he can disappear into (sorry about that, girls). There are the odd few couples who live together in a certain level of harmony all their married lives, so I am told (these must be the ones where the man works away most of the time).

I do not, however, believe that there is such a thing as a married couple who never have any disagreements, as living under the same roof every day of your life with the same person can often lead to petty arguments over the simplest of things, and this is where the ability to hold a conversation often helps.

I find that having a good sense of humour also helps as long as you do not take the piss out of your wife.

I have realised one thing, and that is married life can be simple, it is all down to the man fitting into a woman's life and the woman sorting the man's life out.

The simplest of sentences is also important, as is the ability to say, "Yes, dear." The best piece of advice is to learn when to keep your big mouth shut and by this, I mean shut and shut tight as the slightest word can cause you endless earaches for weeks to come.

One example told to me, the wife buys herself some new clothes and you say that's OK, but then a few days later you decide to buy yourself a fishing rod or something.

When she finds out she does not agree that fishing is essential; she will often let you know that you should not have purchased this item by moaning about it in the usual roundabout way. You will, however, hear about that fishing rod for months, maybe years to come, every single time that she is pissed off with you.

Women can use something against you for ages, long after the man has forgotten all about it, so I'm informed.

Imagine this: you have been married for fifty years and you have upset the wife, sitting watching television and she turns to you and says, "Remember that bloody fishing rod you got thirty years ago."

I have been married to my wife for many years. Yes, most women will feel sorry for her; she is a caring person and my best friend, but if I have ever upset her (which I have quite a lot, so it seems) she lets me know in no uncertain terms and like every woman upon this planet, she can moan and moan and moan as well as the rest of them, and so can we men. So the next time you upset your wife or partner, just remember, instead of trying to backpedal, just walk up to her, kiss her and tell her you are sorry, as it is a hell of a lot easier than living in the doghouse for a week or more, which I expect we deserve.

I often tell my wife that I am sure that men apologise a lot more than women do, and I was advised that women will disagree with my statement, as many women say that men are just misguided in their beliefs. Most males will speak out when they should be trying to keep quiet, and this is why women get the upper hand.

Men often wonder if they would be better off living on their own, but then they think of the pain and upset it would cause themselves to settle down, to continue their day-to-day misery trying to make ends meet, and many of them would miss their maid running around after them, so I am told.

Whilst chatting to a few guys in a pub in Camberley, Surrey, one guy said to me, "Why is there nothing said at the wedding service as to the man doing as he is told for the rest of his married life? Or is it written somewhere in invisible ink that getting married seems to take away the man's right to freedom of speech as well as the right of buying our clothes or having your own opinion?"

Most males and females on this planet will at some point in their lives wish that they could live without their partners. But whilst talking to some ladies during the research of this book, a lady mentioned a saying that I have used quite a lot during my lifetime and it does seem right at this point to add it. "Better the devil you know." And this works both ways.

As with all book writing, researching the subject is essential. I decided to carry this out the old-fashioned way by speaking with hundreds of women and men whilst out shopping and at other events, simply to ask their opinion concerning relationships, and when I approached a woman I was surprised how quickly the husbands/partners returned to their sides to hear what the conversation was about. I found many women were quite frank about their views, at least until the husband got close enough to overhear. This practice was quite normal in reverse as well, but it was quite funny that it was always the guys who said: "Don't tell my wife."

As I was told many years ago, "A man is boss of his own

home, till the wife gets in." Very true.

I often received the comment, "You will never understand a woman," from some men when they realised that I was researching such a book, but it is this type of attitude that leads me to understand why so many women believe men to be stupid, with little or no idea how to act with or towards a woman.

Communication is a massive part of understanding ladies and if you are not willing to communicate with the opposite sex to understand how they feel or how they view situations, and if men are going to spend their lives with this can't-be-bothered attitude, then we deserve what we get. You will be missing many opportunities that may be standing right in front of you, and what can you expect a woman to do, apart from think that you are a complete fool?

One sentence that truly described these types of males was told to me in a supermarket in Camberley, Surrey, by a woman who had just been divorced. It is as follows: "What can you expect when most men let these partners wear the trousers whilst they can only think with their dicks?" Maybe it was not such a well-timed meeting after all, as she did seem a little anti-men at the time, but her statement still held some truth.

Anyway, back to business, where do men go wrong in their relationships? Their main fault is how they start a relationship, as male relationships are mostly based upon sexual attraction and therefore it can place us in an extremely weak position from the start. We are at an instant disadvantage and by the time we find any faults that our partners may have, it is already too late to do anything about it, unless you like spending a lot of time in the doghouse.

Friendships and relationships are a world apart, as a friendship means that you still have some control over when you see this friend, but as emotions take over or sex gets in the way, this weakens the male's position in any relationship and the female then becomes the dominant partner. If at some time you decide to move in together, the rules change yet again and this can often mean that the man needs to rethink his way of life, along with many of his habits.

Many relationships can fail when signs of dominance appear, as most men dislike the feeling of being pushed around or shown up when the partner talks down to him in private or in public. Joint respect is not such a bad thing and this works both ways. Remember, both of you, being with someone, married or just going out, does not mean that you own each other.

The start of any relationship is a major hurdle to anyone, as you may be contemplating whether you are doing the right thing becoming involved with this person, and if he or she is the right one for you. Or should you remain as a free spirit? But it is odd that you hardly ever find fault at the start of a relationship and in some cases, it may be some time before you ask yourself this question.

If you have moved in together and then you are finding yourself in this position, wondering if you should continue in this relationship, do some serious thinking, use some common sense and talk with your partner, taking the time to explain how you are feeling as this can often sort problems before they get out of hand. Maybe they feel the same, but if they do not you can expect a real hard time ahead.

Saying nothing and hoping this problem will just sort itself out and go away will never solve any relationship problems, they just get worse.

Both men and women have their complications and a man will at some time during a relationship think to himself, *Why are women so damn complicated, and why am I the one who is always in the wrong?* The answer is simple: you jumped before thinking, but the lady could be feeling the same.

Now take a step back and think what would have happened here if you had taken the lead in your relationship at the very beginning, talked about working together and settled upon some ground rules between you both. Had been open with each other and showed a mature ability to hold an adult discussion rather than spouting out that you do not like being told what to do, as she will only think that you are an arrogant knob.

The answer is very simple. If you talked and did not like what was said then 'you would have been a lot happier than you are at present, even though you may have still been single'.

Some women can be temptresses as they are fully aware that when they get a male interested in sex they then take control and become the most powerful one in the relationship. Another simple way to explain this is why men chase the opposite sex, yes, you know the answer.

Women tend to say that men do not understand them, but what can women expect when most of what they ask is very equivocal?

The problem men have when in a long-term relationship, is that women have a way of ignoring whatever a man says, their excuse being that men tend to talk a load of rubbish. Then again, the reason could be that women use this ability to shut themselves off as they feel that they know better, therefore ignoring everything we say to them.

How often have you spoken to your partner and she has turned around a couple of seconds later and asked you what you said?

This explains why in many relationships the man will withdraw from the conversation with their partner, as he has gained the view of, "What is the point as she never listens to me anyway?" whilst women do the same. You can say that there is not a great difference between them and men.

Try telling a woman that you will take her out shopping; you will soon get a response.

What makes me laugh is all of these so-called experts who blab on about a man needing to get in touch with his feminine side, but hold on there, do these so-called experts know what they are talking about? NO.

Life has taught men that it is much easier not to question nature or a woman, as there is a good chance that both will go full circle and bite you upon the arse. Many men feel it is just as convenient to keep quiet if you wish an easy life without too much nagging or stress. But times are now changing and women seem more straightforward when you approach them, and you are just as likely to be told to go away, or something along those lines, if they don't want you near them.

5. Consideration & Care

We all know that men and women are often moody, but women have medical terms for this. Research shows that many of the mood cycles are associated with sex hormones and increase before their monthly cycles, but what about all the other times that women have their head from hell on? Well I have been informed that this is still down to certain medical equations, but how come women's moods are all down to medical terms, whilst if a man has a mood on it's because 'he's being an arsehole'? I just wonder, was it a woman doctor that first diagnosed these woman medical problems? It seems that the list is endless: hormonal imbalance, chemical imbalances, menopause, then, of course, there will be pregnancy, hypothyroidism and whatever else they can think up, whilst a man is being, yes, you guessed it, an arsehole. Yes, I am fully aware that many men are standardised as arseholes, but many women could easily fit into this category as well. I know a few ex-partners who are real experts in that field. So what is a guy's excuse?

Then we get women moaning because they feel that life has dealt them a poor hand in many ways. After all, men do not have the worries of monthly cycles or hormones, of course, the endless visits to the hairdressers don't help (that is unless you are a man who is also a bit of a tart himself. I could have added a few names to that list over the years, but I will refrain from doing so).

However, just how complex are the inner workings of a woman compared to that of a man?

Men often catalogue women as the weaker of the sexes. I have done so myself many times during my lifetime. This has to be the biggest mistake a man can make and this has caused the downfall of many men throughout history.

Yes, men including myself have at some time in our lives allowed our private parts to do our thinking for us, only to find out at our own cost that this was not such a good idea.

Have you ever pissed off a woman and lived through it without feeling like you have had your balls put through the financial shredder? If you got away with it, then you can consider yourself a very lucky man, but those of us who were not so lucky will know how it feels.

The best advice that I was ever given was never to underestimate a woman or believe them to be stupid, as you will live to regret this misconception, which can be both expensive and dangerous. I found out with some adverse effects on my financial well-being some years ago that some women in this world are both crafty and manipulative, often looking toward their financial stability rather than a long-term relationship.

The problem any man has is sorting the good women from

the bad ones, but hang on, as this works both ways. There are as many men who will take a woman for everything given the chance as there are women who will take a man for everything.

The following was pointed out to me by a guy at a stag night:

When do you ever hear of a judge awarding a husband a hefty part of a woman's estate in a divorce case? Or is it that news is just not publicised so the guys get more sympathy? This could be why men tend to place all the blame squarely upon the woman in a breakup and vice versa.

On occasion, you may have heard people say, "Behind every successful man there is a woman." Does this mean that the woman gets the credit for the man's success?

But what if the man had been successful before meeting the woman?

Then there is the other question, what happens when a man is not successful? No one makes any comment about a woman being behind the man at this point, but does anyone ever say that behind a successful woman is a man, leading me to believe that he was anti-women or just having a few problems?

I have spent many years of my life with these extremely misunderstood creatures (females) and have witnessed varied areas of the female mind, moods and other tantrums for which the milder sex are so well known (milder sex, no chance). Men always point out this fact, but say nothing about their own faults.

Oh, well, you must always remember that ninety per cent of the time whenever a woman asks a man a question, you can guarantee it will have an alternative meaning, so there is a damn good chance that we men will be wrong no matter what answer is given.

Women who we know and often love are quite capable of using their sexuality to get everything they want, by clicking their fingers or showing a little cleavage, and who can blame them, as most men can be led around by their penises, and some will drop to their knees or run around like lapdogs in the hope of some sexual reward.

Yes, we men are far from perfect, but we feel that we are far less complicated than any females and a lot easier to satisfy. Yes, we males do have a tendency to walk around allowing our penis to think for us, thus often getting us into trouble, but this should be blamed upon advertising, films, and of course, television, as you cannot do anything nowadays without someone shoving sex down your throat and what controls men? Yes, sex.

I also found that many young women stated that they dislike it when older men try to chat them up and the guy gets pissed off when they explain that they are too old, especially when they look older than the young women's fathers.

A few women that I have spoken with said that men are instantly at a disadvantage as we think with our stomachs and dangling bits, and are not able to use our sexuality for manipulation; unlike some women who are capable of turning it off and on when it suits, whilst a male has a very hard time hiding his excitement. (Is that a banana in your pocket?)

But is sex everything it seems to be? An extremely fashionable trend nowadays, or is it that more people have a greater interested in a woman or man's financial well-being, rather than finding out if they are good lovers or good partners?

Shallowness is the fashion of these times. Starting at a very young age, girls seem to be moulded by what they read or view in magazines, on the internet or the television.

It seems that even from school age everything revolves around sex and the number of times that their mates brag that they have been laid, so much so that young girls are becoming sexually aware at very young ages due to the ways that sex sells music, clothes and most other things. It is no wonder that we have so many failings when it comes to relationships and so many underage pregnancies.

Immaturity can be a strong recipe for failing in any relationship, but failing in a relationship does not mean that he or she is a bad person, it could just mean that you are not the right person for each other or the time is not right for you to be together. In fact, it may be a blessing in disguise.

It does not matter if you think that the other person is the right one for you; fate has a way of steering any relationship the way it is destined to go.

It could be the ride of your life (excuse the pun) or the disappointment of your life, but you can be certain that if you are meant to be together, then there is a good chance that you will be and no matter what any scientist has to say upon this statement, fate seems to steer our lives.

One thing you should always do is love, laugh and enjoy life. Even after a disagreement you should kiss and talk about what caused it, in a calm and controlled manner of course.

There are endless matters to take into consideration when starting upon the relationship highway. This could see you both financially and emotionally stable or sad and financially broke; a lot depends upon your choice of partner or career and both of you having the ability to share with each other and be truthful.

Men and women need to understand that a relationship is a two-way street; the male has to be happy as well as the female and so with this in mind, I have tried to show female responses to some of the problems with relationships, sexual problems, and other matters throughout this book.

Many of these answers came from research carried out by myself, which sometimes came close to getting me a smack around the face, for what I would class as no fault of my own.

Men tend to look at women, thinking as men do, *I bet I*

could pull her, but this is where they start upon the wrong road. Firstly men must consider themselves, their actions, their manner, their approach and of course their "CHAT", which is the first thing that we men get wrong. The right way to start is to introduce yourself and if she tells you her name and you start a conversation with her, then ask her what she does for work and get her talking about herself and then shut the hell up and show a real interest in the conversation, as you may find that she possibly warms to you, but if you start giving her "The Man Chat" from the start, you will bore the hell out of her and she will think that you are just another knob on legs.

A woman can read many things into the first few minutes of meeting a guy, but most men are unable to grasp a clear understanding of a woman's body language, as many of us have the problem of our manhood doing our thinking for us and normally it will get it wrong; this will destroy a man's opportunity to make a good impression upon a first meeting and does tend to help the man make a complete and utter idiot of himself, along with any assistance he may have had from alcohol during that day.

Many males grow up with this amazing "Ego" enhancer built in, which seems to start running in overload from a young age. This tells them that every sexy woman they meet will have a strong desire to bed them at the first opportunity, and as many men think that they are irresistible to the opposite sex this will often get them into trouble and can be quite embarrassing at times.

Whilst men get it wrong regularly, many women tend to check men out first, often weighing a man up before any advancement and this process involves many things being considered. Before making any eye contact or approaching him, hair, smile, eyes, build, clothing, shoes, butt and sometimes even the size of his trouser bulge can be under investigation and part of the equation. She may like you and then again, she may not.

The thing that we males must understand is that changing a woman's mind after she has reached her decision is an impossible task, so after she has placed you into a no-go category you have little or no chance of making a difference in her decision, no matter what.

If she has made up her mind that you are a total waste of space and she would be wasting her time upon you, then the sooner you realise and accept it, the easier it becomes to live with the fact that you are not a sex god after all.

Don't be broken-hearted, as the next woman you meet may just be on the same wavelength as you, and you may have to do little or no mental work to get her to like you. This poor woman may not realise what she is letting herself in for.

However, do not rush, just take your time, as there is nothing worse than a man looking desperate in front of a woman, thus giving the woman the upper hand.

Try to look as if you are at peace with your present situation, but not so peaceful that the poor woman has trouble staying awake, as this can make you look like a total idiot, which will force the woman to look for ways to leave as soon as possible.

One saying I always hated is, "Beauty is only skin deep." I expect the person who started this statement was as ugly as hell; anyway, nobody wants to wake up beside an ugly person. But even ugly people have feelings, so next time an ugly person asks you out try to let them down slowly by being friendly and always remember, beauty is only skin deep, and this means that shouting rude obscenities at the top of your voice to make yourself look big in front of your mates may be slightly over the top. Remember that beauty is only skin deep.

Some men and women tend to show off when they are out with mates. All they want is a laugh and to get pissed even if this may seem audacious to others, but why should they care? "It's a laugh, after all." Then they wonder why nice women steer clear of them as if they were carriers of some disease.

This is a subject called "stupidity" or sometimes related to being immature, but hopefully, they will grow out of that someday, as it does nothing for their street credibility or their chance of finding a decent partner.

It's like those crowds of guys who used to go to watch a movie at my local cinema and no sooner had the movie started, they started throwing things at the girls sitting downstairs to get their attention, and they wondered why the girls were not interested, and it is still the same today.

Maturity is something that "sometimes" comes with age.

Many women do not want a guy who acts like a ten-year-old when he is around his mates or her. She wants someone who she feels safe with and will enjoy going out with, someone who cares how she feels about their relationship and shows that they feel the same.

But, remember that the possibility of meeting someone is greater when you are not looking for someone.

Quote

After winning an argument with your partner, the best thing a man can do is apologise as soon as possible.

(Note supplied by Joy Edwards)

Never judge an attractive woman as untouchable, as many beautiful women are looking for a man who is himself a nice person. This means that you do not have to be a film-star lookalike or have the body of a god; she wants a loving person who will love her for herself and not for her looks.

But always remember, just because a woman makes eye contact and says "hello" when passing, this does not mean that she wants to bed you. It could be that she is just a polite, friendly person.

However, if a woman is interested in you she may be the

one to make the first move, maybe she will even go as far as flirting a little but take it easy, "lover boy", as she may be trying to get to know a little more about you, and if you move in too fast you may well scare her off.

Most men have never really understood the concept of body language and how it works and have often deemed it simply stupid, which is how we men explain things when we cannot grasp a sensible explanation. But the more that I have read about body language, I have found that the facts speak for themselves, meaning that if men took the time to visit the hundreds of body language sites upon the internet, then there is a good chance that they could find some assistance.

These were just a few pointed out to me:

If she hangs around a while and it seems that urgency is not important, turn the conversation away from you and get her to talk about herself. Make sure to show that you are genuinely interested in what she has to say. Do not interrupt her whilst she is speaking; allowing a woman to talk about herself will score you some serious bonus points, as many women like good manners in a man.

There are some signs to look out for as well, for example, if she is close to you and she leans forward as if to get closer, this shows that she is attracted to you and if she starts to whisper in your ear, she is telling you that she wants to be even closer. Your move.

When seated, if she crosses her legs towards you, this should mean that she wants you to stay where you are, but if she starts to swing her leg in a kicking motion then I am sorry to say you are getting the boot. (So bye-bye, better luck next time.)

Other signs to look out for are:

She makes direct steady eye contact. You can encourage her by returning a few lingering gazes, but if you overdo it this will make her uncomfortable. Always watch where your line of vision is (not below the neck).

If she shows both rows of teeth when you first meet then she is pleased to see you.

There are certain hair movements which are also flirtatious and can show that the woman fancies you. If she touches or flicks her hair, this is called "preening", which means "admiring and cleaning oneself", but this does not mean grabbing her hand and dragging her upstairs or behind a bush.

If she tilts her head and looks at you in a sultry manner, this can also mean that she is interested in you.

I have heard it said that up to 80% of what we communicate is non-verbal. There are many different actions and gestures (body language) that a woman can carry out without saying a single word that will show you if she is for or against you getting closer to her. Men need to learn and understand that women can think for themselves, and can judge a man a whole lot better than a man can judge a woman. One of the biggest turn-offs for a woman is a man bragging (telling lies) or showing off to her.

So do your research about body language.

Men know that women are normally quite easy to watch, but they seem oblivious to the idea of women giving them a clue through the use of body language.

Keep calm, giving the lady a chance to get to know you a little better, so she can relax and feel at ease in your company.

There are so many sites upon the internet which cover the subject of understanding body language but I have only touched the surface and due to comments made to me during endless talks I have held with parties of people, I would strongly suggest that you take the time and try to do your research. Get some understanding concerning your approach to women and ways to speak to them. Remember, they are human beings after all.

They are not just there for sex or for a man to take his anger out on and if a woman enjoys your company and she wants to be with you, then that is a start. Remember, a woman will make love to you when she is ready to do so and if you are the man to whom she wants to make love.

Be gentle, share the moment and enjoy the time with her. Never should you force yourself upon a woman, drunk or sober.

Yes, sex is enjoyable, but it seems that there is no longer any mystery left as when you meet certain women, the goods are all on show for everyone to see. Many females nowadays go out clubbing or to the pub with their implanted boobs and pumped-up arses hanging out (all in the name of fashion). It is at this point that the older generation has heart attacks or strokes or simply thinks, *Oh my god.*

These women/girls may think they look good, but many men will view them as salacious and resign themselves to stay well clear. Of course, there will always be those men who think to themselves that they are guaranteed to be laid tonight and this is a present-day problem, as fucking upon the first date seems to be a common practice and this may be why sexually transmitted infections are rampant nowadays.

It does seem that many women and men dress to capture, with the view of having sex by the end of the evening. I think many of us have done it.

But if sex is the only thing that they go on the hunt for, I hope that safe sex is their practice. It may be great sex, but this is an unsuitable footing for a steady relationship due to the possibility that there will be a capricious view toward trust between them.

However, it has been pointed out to me that as some men and women believe they are gods to the opposite sex and class themselves as irresistible, we must not be too judgemental thinking that the fault is with one person, as often many people are just as bad as each other.

Nevertheless, if all of the goods are on show and that is how they wish to live their lives, maybe one day they will come to their senses before it is too late, as a little pride in one's appearance is nothing to be ashamed of and many men like a little mystery. What's the saying? "If it looks and acts like a tart, then more than likely is a tart." This applies to both sexes.

As with all men, women come in all different sizes and ages and I think that you may agree with me that if they were all the same, then life would be very boring.

Take care, as not all those women or men who look so sweet and innocent are sweet or innocent, and I am sure that you may find this out later, but if you do try your luck and get a smack around the face, this could be a possible sign that you read it wrong again.

The fact is that many common relationships start auspiciously upon sex and often break up after a short time due to a lack of maturity upon one or both sides, or simply because the sex became boring, which brings about many of the arguments and thus causes a downward spiral, often contributed to by jealousy or infidelity by one or both partners. The bottom line is that we live in a sleep-around society, where sexually transmitted diseases are greatly on the increase and if you do not practice safe sex then it is only a matter of time before your sloppy lifestyle will catch you up. But I do not intend to preach. Oops.

Some friends can be a source of good advice if they have known you for some time, and if they tell you to stay well clear of certain females or males take notice and ask why. Men are very poor at listening and at the slightest flash of cleavage, fail to take notice of any advice no matter how well-meaning it may be. This has happened to many of us, and a few weeks later you find yourself with a problem.

If you find yourself in this position and you tackle the person about it you can guarantee that you get a sob story from them. Don't believe it.

This shows just how stupid humans can be, as we get a warning, then still go ahead and do what nature intended us to do, all because they looked nice and with a male, it would be thinking with your appendage again.

All I can say is, if you try and they allow you on the first date, then ask yourself this question: how many others have been there before you? Remember that the fault is not only with the woman here, as many men have the same view, so this is not one-sided.

The advice that was given to me years ago was as follows:

Many people go through life with a blinkered attitude and a short-sighted view of their future. Picking up a sexually transmitted disease is a lot easier than you think and can leave you sterile and unable to have a family in the future.

I was always told, "Don't take a chance, take a precaution as a safety measure."

The one subject that came up during many conversations was the subject of infections picked up after a partner has played away from home, and then the disagreements between partners as the guilty partner always blames the other, thus causing a total breakdown and end to the relationship.

Upsetting as it may seem, it does allow the innocent partner the chance to understand how disloyal the other partner has been, unless they have been doing the same, of course.

Although most men realise that they will encounter stressful situations in their relationships at some time or another, they continue their endeavours to become emotionally involved with these somewhat mystifying creatures of the opposite sex at any opportunity that is offered to them.

It does not matter how hard a man tries to gain the upper hand in a relationship, a woman often ends up holding us men by the wedding tackle. Surely this is the main reason we spend so much of our time agreeing with them, simply to keep the peace and save us from yet another ear-bashing.

I am, however, informed (by a lady of course) that this is no longer the 1960s and a man does not have the right to rule over a woman's life. This is not always the case, as she knew of many occasions when the male turned out to be the dominant partner. I think that it is a case of men tending to give up after a short period together (or married) so we can gain a little peace. (I am informed by my wife that the reason we agree is simply that the woman is always right. Simple female thinking.) I believe a simpler answer is, "What else can you expect when women have all the right equipment to wrap us men around their little fingers?" and we fall for it every single time.

This is why men fail; we know that if we upset our lady we will miss out on sex for a while and as we men are mostly motivated by sex, this seems to be one of the ways a dominating female can get back at us. Also an easy way for her to get her way. Surely, boys, this shows that we men can understand the female mind on some occasions, but fail to take action with the knowledge that we have, and you can be sure if this happens once, then she will use this ploy again. An easy way around it is to spoil her by buying some flowers or something she likes, just to help steer her mood, but be warned, no man can tell how long this good mood will last, or what we may say or do to destroy it.

There are occasions (which I have covered in this book) where the one being controlled does not realise how manipulative the other partner is, in the early stages of their relationship, and fails to act earlier to solve the problem, therefore chances of a happy relationship with this partner are certain to end.

It seems, therefore, that in some relationships it is possible for a dominant partner to be suffering from NPD and not wishing to change, as they do not believe that they have anything wrong with themselves. It is their partner who's in the wrong. But if this is the case then there is little or no possible way that you can change them on your own.

You should know by their attitude that you are wasting your time and if you have suffered unhappiness over a long period due to this problem, it may be worth giving up as the behaviour problems can be far deeper than you know.

It is a fact that a controlling personality like this can break down the other partner's confidence a little at a time over a period until the partner feels worthless and still does not realise that there is something wrong.

Some controlling partners will go out of their way to manipulate everyday situations, thus allowing them to blame their partner for the slightest thing and enforcing their control. This is mostly carried out so that the weaker partner begins to question their inner self or their behaviour, often deeming that they are the cause of the problems within the home.

Those with this nature could not survive if they had to control their own life without doing so through another person, but they fail to see any fault in their actions.

A man or woman often allows this poor treatment to continue as finding ways to fit in with their partner's disorder is a much easier way to keep the peace, and the non-dominant partner will often blame themselves.

If you happen to be in a controlled relationship, you may not even realise it, as it can take many forms, as simple as a put-down, where they are making decisions on your behalf, calling you an idiot in front of friends, always having to be right, telling you what you can buy or where to spend your money, not allowing you out without knowing where you are at all times, and going so far as making it very hard or nearly impossible to see friends and family.

Remember, love is all about sharing and that does not mean giving up everything you enjoy so your partner can have their way. This also means that they do not make all of the decisions in your relationship, as this should be a partnership.

There can be many hardships in dealing with a partner, but if you happen to get one who is in the relationship solely for personal gain with little or no feelings for you, then you have trouble on your hands. It is extremely hard to find out if they are using you. The main problem is that many women have come to realise men can be easily manipulated, simply because not all men think with their heads. After all, a woman only has to make you think that she is interested and the game is on. Some women will even go as far as to use sex to play you, but by using common sense you will get some idea of her intentions after a short time with her.

She may tell you that she is interested when you ask or

even tell you that she loves you, but eventually starts to show certain signs that should warn you otherwise. These can be simple things like, she does not return telephone calls, she is only interested when you buy her things, when she talks about the plans she is making for the future they do not include you, and she makes you feel like she would prefer to be elsewhere.

Some men can do this a lot with older women, those who are lonely and looking for love. They sell the idea of being in love with her, then comes the hard-luck story to get her money.

Tread carefully and never tell people that you are financially stable and what your bank account holds.

This is what men think that they need to be:

DO YOU MEN FIT INTO ANY OF THESE CATEGORIES?
WITHOUT FORGETTING TO:
1. Give her compliments, regularly
2. Love to go shopping
3. Be honest
4. Be relatively rich
5. Not stress her out
6. Not look at other women

AND AT THE SAME TIME, YOU MUST ALSO:

1. Give her lots of attention, but expect little yourself
2. Give her lots of time, especially time for herself
3. Give her lots of space, never worrying about where she goes or who she is with

BUT IT IS ALSO VERY IMPORTANT TO:

Never forget: birthdays, anniversaries

* Arrangements she makes * her parents

A WOMAN HAS TO BE ALL THOSE THINGS AND OFTEN A MAN'S:

1. Mother
2. Cook
3. Cleaner
4. Babysitter/Child Minder
5. Nurse
6. Food Shopper
7. Taxi Driver after a night out with the boys
8. Excuse Maker
9. Maid
10. Sometimes a Punchbag

The Punchbag was added simply as it seems some so-called men are in relationships where they feel that they have a right to bunch, beat up or threaten their wives or girlfriends. I simply class these as lesser men, or Microdicks as a woman said to me.

6. Understanding

There are hundreds, maybe thousands of people who have knowledge in relationships around the world. Those people understand emotions, sex, moods, love, hate, clothes and whatever else that they can think up to make themselves money, but no matter what, they all come to the same conclusion, which seems to be that "men and women are different, whilst being the same". What in the hell does that mean? All I can tell you is, "some of them know or understand sweet nothing".

Learning from books at school has nothing to do with living the journey.

The only way to understand relationships, love and marriage is by living them.

Any man or woman can tell you that both sexes are different from each other in so many ways and you do not need to be an expert in anything to understand that. They have different emotions, moods, tastes in clothes and often view many love/hate situations differently, so why do people need so-called experts to state something which common sense can tell you? Each male and female differs from the next male and female, and so on.

What applies to both men and women is that some do not wish to get involved emotionally, whilst others cannot wait to marry the first person they meet. Those who jump into a relationship too quickly may, however, find it to be a fatal mistake. Taking a little time to think things through can often save you a lot of anguish later. Foresight can be a wonderful thing, but most times a person's heart can rule their head, or in most men's cases, it will be their penis who thinks for them.

In any relationship, one of the most important things is getting to know each other, but you can be certain that you will never really know somebody properly within the first six months, or until you have your first real argument, as it is at this point that their real personality will come shining through and you may not like what you see. This will be the time to ask yourself if you believe that you have any future with this person, or will you still feel the same in another six months? Remember that if someone tells you that they are sorry repeatedly, can you really believe them again?

But if you are in a rocky relationship where there are endless arguments, ask yourself, "Is it sensible to think about marriage or planning to have a baby?" If you are willing to end your independence just because you slept with this person then you are not thinking straight. After all, falling in love too easily is for fools and can be very expensive in the end. I can assure you, repeat apologies mean nothing.

Some relationships can end upon amicable terms when both partners realise that they are not going anywhere with each other, but what happens if you're not compatible and it all ends in a shouting match? You guys must always remember the following saying: "Hell hath no fury like a woman scorned," as this has to be one of the best pieces of advice anyone can give. Guys who get a Dear John can be arses too.

Whilst everything is moving along smoothly and the relationship is great, loving and without any hitches, you'll feel as if the world is full of roses and you're walking on air, but then, most of us can relate to a time when a partner has said to you, "I think that we need to have a break for a while." What this normally means is that they have someone else waiting to take your place. Using this bullshit, "I feel we need to take a break for a short time," is because they don't have the guts to just say, "Get lost," or, "Fuck off," as simple as that. Why can't people be honest?

Now try to leave with your dignity intact and remember that they are the loser, as quite often these new relationships fail quite quickly and they will wish that they had remained with you, but by then you hopefully will have moved on and found someone new.

If it is a joint decision then that is fine, but what happens when the guy gets fed up and suggests that you take a break from each other? The guy becomes the biggest bastard on the planet and is hated by the ex-partner along with all of her friends. Without any doubt, I can guarantee that with the support of her friends she will go for your throat at the very first chance. Or another part of your anatomy, given the chance.

Some men and women turn into complete psychos when they split with a partner and it always seems to end up being the fault of the other person. Sometimes it may be, but then again, this is a breakup for you. Don't get me wrong, as many people split up with an ex and remain friends.

It amazed me how so many men have pointed out that a woman is a combination of many different emotions ranging from sensitive, sexy, loving and caring, where you cannot wait to be with her and hold her in your arms, then just wait till an argument starts and she can turn into a real red-eyed she-devil, bitchy, nasty and evil, but is the guy being a gentleman during any disagreement?

Women are well known for suffering from the mysterious effect of the instant mood swing, which takes place in a split second and seems to always have a man upon the receiving end, but the worst thing about being a man at this time is that she normally goes after your nuts, and I do not mean the ones squirrels eat. I realise that many of these comments were one-sided, as many women stated that commenting about this matter would be below them, as men make these comments without any firm evidence. But we men admit that we can be as bitchy as any woman can.

Men's main problem is that we are incapable of learning from mistakes, which often drops us into the crap with partners and causes us to become confused as to how we got into this position and how these female moods work.

We are, however, fully aware of the fact that whatever goes wrong, we men are normally upon the receiving end of a woman's bad mood and being blamed for causing them, even though we are being cursed for something we may not have the slightest clue as to what we have done to cause.

Men know that women are always saying one thing, whilst their actions contradict their words. Seemingly it is the male in any relationship that is kept in the dark, whilst being blamed for most things that go wrong.

I feel that as all men are born without the ability to read a woman's mind and as we are not supplied with an all-seeing crystal ball at birth, we must try to get a better understanding of the confusion that we feel must be going on inside a female head. This confusion, which they call 'female understanding or female intuition' seems to control everything that puts us men in the frame for blame. Remember, when she tells you that nothing is wrong, it normally means that everything's wrong, at which point you should take the hint and shut the hell up, as taking the matter any further will only get you into deeper trouble. It does not matter how many times you ask her what is the matter, the answer will always be the same: "You just don't understand me," or, "I told you before."

The truth here is that men cannot read a female's mind, so how in the hell will we understand what is wrong when we don't try?

A woman once told me that the difference between a man and a woman is simple: "Men are born with testicles, whilst women are born with a conscience." Yet another harsh female statement to undermine a man's credibility, I expect, but ask yourself, could it be true that we men cause most of the problems in our partnerships? Maybe this is the reason our "dangling bits" are always commented about and blamed for getting us men into so much trouble during our lifetime.

Surely understanding why women point out our "dangling bits" as the problem starter may just be part of the solution to understanding women. It could just be jealousy on behalf of the women that they were not supplied with "dangling bits" in the beginning, but if they were I expect we men would be redundant in the bedroom department.

Now, the thing that can multiply the problem, is if a woman has had a bad experience whilst in a relationship. This may be a reason for some mistrust of men and their "dangling bits". This will always be the case if men refuse to take notice of what is going on around them and are unwilling to communicate with the females in their lives.

Many people I have spoken to believe that most men and women have their lives already planned out from a young age, which nowadays seems to be mostly financially motivated in many cases, whilst hoping and praying that a special person with loads of cash will come along or their hard work and dedication will advance them enough financially to maintain a friendship with a male solely upon their terms. Many men still think these female plans could not be put into action without the assistance of one or more of us gullible, easily led males who still think that members of the female population need them.

We spend most of our lives hunting for the so-called perfect woman, with the hope of spending the rest of our lives in harmony with her, then later we spend the remainder of our years trying to escape from her. What in the hell have we men ever done to deserve this punishment? Mother Nature must have a real downer on men.

Surely a little more relaxation would be nice. If you are married and reading this you will know that 90% of the time, as soon as you sit your arse into a chair the wife will call you with something to do and it seems that this does not change, no matter how long you are married.

Now just take a second to ask yourself this one simple question.

When you got together with your lady, was it because you no longer had your mother around to pick up after you or wipe your backside? It seems that so many men get together with a partner so he has someone to wait upon him hand, foot, and finger.

All men agreed that they love beautiful women, but

nowadays it seems to be going overboard with implants and plastic.

If a relationship is on its last legs and it's heading for the toilet, often both partners find it hard to communicate in any reasonable way with each other. Harsh words and bad language can often be the format of exchanged words and thoughts of getting out or being with someone else can often be the cause, but you should think back to when you were in love at one point and maybe take the lead, calming down, whilst acting with a little restraint.

One of the biggest mistakes can be to tell your friends that you will be breaking up before you tell your partner, as this should remain private till the end, otherwise there is a damn good chance of this coming back and biting you upon the arse.

We have all had breakups with ex-partners (that's why they are ex-partners) but it is never an easy thing to do and finding the right moment is so hard unless you are in the middle of a flaming argument, then you can use this time to simply drop the bomb.

Breaking the news should be done away from the place where you have been living so that your partner does not have anything to throw at you. Remember that it will hurt no matter how you say it, especially if one of you is not expecting it.

Breaking up with a partner is hard, but many of us have never been able to tolerate women or men who rewrite the history of their relationship just because they refuse to accept any responsibility for predicaments they get themselves into, often blaming the other partner for any and every situation that is brought about by their stubbornness when they refuse to take any advice, sometimes going as far as inventing lies to make the other partner look bad so they gain sympathy.

Now you must ask yourself this: is the real truth that men bring about the problems themselves and place the blame upon the women just to save themselves from facing the truth? Or is it that women go out of their way to create problems just so they can point the finger at men to help them to feel superior?

Years ago, when you broke up with a partner it took time for the news to circulate as friends told other friends and eventually it died out, but with the introduction of social media websites the problems get far greater coverage and you can be publicly humiliated in front of the whole school or workplace all at the same time. The lies told can be quite soul-destroying.

I can never see the point of trying to humiliate someone when a relationship ends, as their friends believe them and your friends believe you, so what do you gain? But when it gets to a level where a child is involved and used by one of the parents as a tool to hurt the other, I honestly think that the parent should be locked away from society so the child does not have contact with them, otherwise the child grows up being as evil as the parent, thinking that their behaviour is quite natural, and any lies or nasty tricks are part of the child's way of life, as trained by their parent.

This is far too often an event in society today and not just a story in a book.

Women often become irritated or moody seemingly for no reason, and often blame the men in their lives, so this leads men to believe that they can never do anything right.

Yes, many of us have experienced this behaviour and it is at this point you have to step back and think to yourselves, *Have I missed something?* A special day, birthday, wedding anniversary or the day you first met? Something that you arranged or promised.

This list could be endless so keeping a diary, entering alarms upon your mobile or simply getting the wife to leave a message on your phone are easy ways to help. We men are not very good at remembering things such as wedding anniversaries and for this reason, we should be given a break. (This is solely a man's view.)

But can it be that simple? Sorry to say, it is not. Sometimes you can be in the doghouse for no particular reason and it can be as simple as someone pissed the misses off today and you are the one who normally gets it in the rear end.

Do not try to be smart as it will come back to haunt you.

Women are a law unto themselves and nature must have

had a real laugh when putting them together. Just as you think you know and understand their ways, they are throwing a fit and you are the one in trouble. Speaking your mind will only land you in further trouble, so keep it shut if you wish to sleep in your bed again.

Some men find comfort in football and beer, whilst some others are in the arms of another woman (they must be mad). But does this solve the problem? No.

The reason is that football ends and you still have to return home at the end of the match. Whilst pubs may stay open a little longer there is a limit that every drinker can consume or afford, and returning home pissed out of your mind will never assist with your problem or the woman's mood.

The thought of getting involved with another woman means you are just opting for one problem over another and possibly opening a whole new assortment of problems.

One guy told me that he and his wife had a massive disagreement and he went around to see an ex-girlfriend so he could get out of the house and stayed the night. The problem was that this old friend had changed her job and was now working in the same company as his wife, and the next day she went straight to his wife and told her. Next thing his wife hit him with a divorce and cleaned him out. Sorry, guys, but I'm on her side.

The only way to resolve a problem is to face it head-on and find out what caused the problem in the first place.

Now step very carefully as this can also backfire upon you. Some couples believe that by ignoring a problem, it will go away, but let me tell you, it never does.

Hundreds of marriages fail each year as couples are far too self-opinionated, stubborn, or just unable to do such a simple thing as talking to each other.

Another bad thing is listening to advice from girlfriends and mates as this can make the hole that you are in so much deeper. The settee is not a nice long-term option, and neither is spending any period in the same house with a person who does not wish to speak with you, I can confirm from experience.

Remember, when you start a relationship your lady may tell you that she would "never want to change you". Keep that in mind as if you ever marry her, sooner or later she will try to change everything about you. After all, she is a woman.

Looks seem to be the flavour of choice nowadays, with people being very shallow and self-centred.

Men are looking for the ultimate bed partner, normally with good looks and a lovely body, whilst many women look for the tall, handsome man with muscles. The problem is that being over-judgemental concerning a person's looks can be extremely superficial and a short-lived answer to your compatibility, as time changes most things and everyone's body tends to spread and head for the floor. Anyway, who says that the outer cover of this beauty does not hide a nasty person within?

Relationships are normally built over time and many of us may not realise that the person we are seeing may not be our soul mate.

Partnerships can be as simple as a chance meeting that has created a spark, and then you have parted with a strong feeling that you were just meant for each other, but this is not always the case. Only if you are lucky.

Often it can be as easy as bumping into someone, but the harder you try to find that special person, the harder it becomes to find them, so live your life and if it is meant to be, they will come along.

I met my wife twenty-eight years ago and she is still putting up with me all these years later. Even now, we remain friends, but we laugh a lot and if we do have any problems we will say to the other one that we need to have a chat and it is as simple as that, which is quite an achievement as there is an age gap of twenty years.

As I have mentioned so many times throughout these pages, being able to talk to your partner openly and express how you feel without the other partner throwing a fit is the best way to deal with problems, and this is how you start your relationship and continue to maintain it over the years, along with lots of love and kisses.

If you have any problems and are worried about anything, the longer you ignore it the harder you will find it is to openly speak to your partner about it.

If you allow it to get to the stage where you can't talk to each other without getting into an argument or you cannot stand the other person touching you or being next to you, then it is time to seek help or simply call it a day and move on with your life.

But talking to others, such as friends, is something that I refuse to do as I tried it many years before I met my present wife, and by listening to friends and work colleagues I ended up with a very nasty divorce, and the only people who gained were solicitors.

I often asked myself after the divorce where I went wrong and the answer was simply, I took the advice of idiots who had suffered from bad breakups and had gotten well and truly burnt themselves.

So I say, "Do not listen to friends or workmates."

If you wish, you can seek advice through a marriage guidance counsellor or relationship specialist, go ahead, but many of these people can be unmarried or read advice from books with absolutely zero experience of marriage or relationships or dealing with problems between couples.

I was told a many years ago to speak with an old woman who lived near me when having problems and so I went along to see her, and the first thing that she asked me was if I had spoken to my partner about the problems and how I felt things between us were going wrong.

I spent an hour or more chatting with this lady who was eighty-eight years of age and had been married for over sixty years, but sadly lost her husband two years previously.

I was amazed at the advice that this lady had for me and the way that she understood why her happy married life had lasted so long. The answer was simply being able to talk to each other and she added that this was made easier as they never own a television at any time during their lifetime.

I returned home and sat for a couple of hours talking with my wife and everything returned to normal, and this is how life works things out – talking.

Most of us have suffered from weight gain or illness during our lives, sometimes brought about by our home, job or relationships and this can be a stumbling point for many of us. Whilst some people feel that life is letting them down and they continually worry about not having someone to love or share their lives with.

As a real friend, you worry that if you tell them the reason they fail to attract anyone is simply their appearance, they could be emotionally hurt and as many people do not wish to hurt their friends' feelings by stating the obvious, it can be one of the hardest steps to take. Well sometimes you have to be cruel to be kind, or do you?

When someone lets themselves go it can be for so many different reasons, a relationship breakup or some bad news where they feel that their life is just not worth anything.

Then again, it can be as simple as there is nothing wrong,

but the person does not realise that the way they dress does not come across in the same way as they see their outfit in the mirror. For example: a woman could think that she looks good when she dresses in a provocative manner whilst her friends think that she could easily be mistaken for a prostitute.

Some walk around thinking that they are so beautiful when more often than not, a man will look at them and feel repulsed.

Most people would love to have that special someone upon their arm or beside them on cold lonely nights, but come on, people, nobody wants to wake up beside a male or female Godzilla.

One thing that many men and women pointed out that should be taken into consideration is a person's pride in their appearance. A number of people seem to let themselves go as soon as they settle into a relationship; so many men and women who used to play sport just stop as soon as they find a partner who would prefer to spend their time stretched out upon the sofa slowly becoming yet another victim of a heart attack. Remember, being a slob is not doing you or your love life any favours. How can someone fancy you when you go from Wow to Whopper. Even though there are many of those who adore people with weight problems, all the big friends that I have known over the years had a far greater sense of humour compared to the thin ones that I knew, and supporting someone to lose weight is being a true friend, as you could be saving their life.

When out shopping at the supermarket with my wife, I often see people supporting an overweight waistline along with an overloaded trolley closely followed by their husband/partner, supporting a large gut.

It is at this point a certain question comes into my head. "Will they be around in a year or two?" The answer is no if they don't change their lifestyle.

Life is often a serious let-down. As we get older and look into the mirror, we fail to see the truth looking back at us. Often the person we see is a younger, more virile version of what we are and this thought seems to give your ego that little extra boost, but as this country has a massive problem with obesity, those who do nothing about their problem are only heading towards an early death, so now it is time for that kick up the arse you have been awaiting for such a long time. You are unhappy, but why are you unhappy?

Do something about it before it kills you. Remember, you can only live life to the full if you are fit enough to do so.

There is nothing worse than your children or family watching someone they love or care for go from a smiling happy person to a sad shell, so think about your future.

Keeping the ability to talk openly to family and being truthful with your partner and friends is and always will be the best action that you can take, often meaning that both of you will be able to openly share your thought and concerns with each other, knowing that neither will be upset by the other's truthful advice.

Life is strange in lots of ways. For example, you split from your partner and all your friends tell you to get out and find someone else, as there are plenty more fish in the sea.

Sometimes you feel like your heart has been so badly broken that all you want to do is die. Most of us know how that feels, as many males and females have been in this position and never thought that we would pull through, but we did, and now we can look back and think of how it taught us to understand that jealousy is a nasty thing.

Jealousy (The Green-Eyed Monster) is one of the biggest destroyers of relationships. Sometimes it is a boost to your ego when your partner starts to show signs of jealousy; it can soon become outweighed by fights and resentment that can float to the surface, but sometimes it can be caused by hearing that your partner has been seen with another person of the opposite sex and the reason can be completely innocent.

However, if jealousy continues in a relationship, it will become impossible to control or suffer as time passes, often leading to violent outbursts and regular assaults and at this point, it is time to get out.

The only problem is, the longer that you put up with a jealous person, the harder it becomes to break up as the bond becomes stronger over time, but if there is violence in a relationship, it does not matter how long you have been together – get out and stay out.

Jealousy is not something that affects only a man, as it is as much a problem for some women as well.

Many men and women stay in a jealous relationship simply because they tell themselves that they will get better, but that is not going to happen. Jealousy is the hardest emotion to control and that is speaking from experience.

One guy I spoke with told me when he was in his early twenties, he was a sufferer of extreme jealousy and it was so bad that he would cross a street and have a go at someone, as he thought that the guy was "eyeing up" his girlfriend at the time. The only thing he achieved because of jealousy was that he lost his girlfriend, as she was sick of his behaviour. Who could blame her?

Jealousy is often called the Green-Eyed Monster and there is a very good reason for it to have that name, so think twice next time you have jealous thoughts. If the girl or boy you are with wanted to be with someone else, then they would not be with you.

Grow up and act your age, not your shoe size.

Remember to make your relationship a pleasure to be in. Share the good times and make them last most of the time.

Relationships have often been described as a two-way street and the only way to make them work, is by working together as a team. Working as a team means that you cannot expect everything your way. No matter if you are 16, 26, or 60, treat your partner like someone special and stop taking liberties. Wanting them to give in to your needs and wants all the time is just acting like a spoilt child.

Whenever possible, do something out of the normal just to add a little spark to your relationship and remember, laughing is great medicine. Even when short of money or down upon your luck, the joy that laughing can bring lifts you up out of the gloom and makes you feel better for a while.

There is a saying: "remember that there is always someone worse off than yourself".

Well, life often catalogues women as the weaker of the sexes; I have done so myself. This has also been the cause of the downfall of many men. "Yes, men," and this includes most of us, have at some time in our lives allowed our private parts to do our thinking for us, as I stated before, only to find out at our own cost that this was not such a good idea.

The best advice that I was given is to never underestimate a woman or believe them to be stupid, or you may live to regret this misconception. This can be both expensive and dangerous. I found out with some adverse effects on my financial well-being that some women are both crafty and manipulative, often looking toward their financial stability rather than a long-term relationship. Remember, I did say "some women".

Most males will suffer the wrath of a woman sometime during their life, and this can be an extremely disturbing experience, often leaving you shaken for some time or unsure about relationships or commitment for life. Humans are one of the only species on this planet that I believe can smile and be pleasant to your face, whilst kicking you in the gut and clearing out your bank balance at the same time, but I am sure that this has happened to many men and women.

Married life, or simply living together, is and always will be hard, as another human being with a completely separate personality has invaded your personal space and this personality is bound to clash with your own at certain times. At these times, it becomes very stressful to share that space. I have always found that a hobby or other interest such as sport or fishing can relieve a lot of the stress before you both get to the stage of killing each other. (Another woman is not an option here.) But remember that too much of another interest outside your home can also cause problems, as some women have this idea that if you live together then you should have some say upon what you can or can't do. Remember that this can also work in reverse.

Some men will let their partner have their way, ruling the home just to keep the peace and allow themselves an easy life. This is pure fantasy as there must be ground rules in any relationship, otherwise eventually one of the partners starts to hold a grudge against the other and failure to solve this can cause it to bring extreme pressure upon an already stressed relationship, and can push one of the partners into the arms of another person.

Marrying a younger person can often bring many problems too. The fact that there is a generation gap of whatever years is the start of some of the problems. If the man is older, he will often be like a father figure to the woman. This is quite a strain upon a relationship and this fact also relates to the older woman marrying the younger guy.

Many younger men and women marry older partners in the hope that they will have greater financial stability, but often find that this is not the case, or the difference in ages create a lot more stress. However, not everyone is in it for financial gain.

Overall, many mistakes can be solved by speaking to each other, as stated previously, but what happens when the age gap is the problem and the older person views the younger one's behaviour as childish or immature? Well, you have to explain how you feel, as I am sure nobody can really read minds.

Boredom is another reason one partner finds enjoyment with another man or woman. When the spark has gone out of a relationship you will find little or no enjoyment in being with your partner.

One sign of a possible breakup can your partner seemingly pointing out your faults at any opportunity, but what happens if this role is reversed?

Some of these faults can be: your driving, the way you dress, the way you eat or speak and even the way that you act. Nothing seems to be of a suitable standard for them anymore and this is the time when you feel that you cannot take much more of it. If you fail to talk to each other about this and other matters, things will only become worse, until the damage is beyond repair, then you need to call time and move on with your life, as what is the point of both of you feeling tied down and constantly miserable? Life is for living and at this point, neither of you are doing much living...

Many years ago I was in this situation and had become so despondent about the future that I was willing to try anything to get this relationship back on track, so I invited my then partner at the time (as we had split up) out for a meal to clear the air. The evening went off well with decent conversation and we seem to be getting on quite well, for a change.

At the end of the evening, I dropped her back at her place and drove home by myself.

The next day I received a call from her asking me if I would like to come over that night for dinner and I accepted.

I arrived at her house (a house that had been paid for with my money). She opened the door, gesturing for me to enter and she was quite friendly.

She told me to remove my coat and get a beer, which I did

not, and informed her that I was working later, but the evening continued with a friendly conversation.

The meal was individual home-made meat pies with mash, carrots and peas, which I must say was the best meal that this woman had ever made. After the meal, I said that I had to go, thanked her and turned to leave, at which point she said, "I hope that you enjoyed the dog food."

I thought she was just mucking around until she showed me a tin of Chum.

All I could say was, "That must be why it was an improvement on your normal cooking," and walked out the door, got in my car and drove away. As soon as I got far enough out of sight I stopped the car and (excuse the pun), I was as sick as a dog.

After that evening I could not stand to communicate with the bitch. Just this one old bike from life.

I was always told that some people bring sunshine into your life when they enter, whilst others do so when they leave. She was 100% upon leaving.

I have not tried any dog food since.

Arguments and disagreements can often start over the most trivial reasons and sometimes continue for days. Some arguments start from comments made by friends or family members and this has happened to most of us.

Mothers often lay the foundations for relationship

problems, as they believe that their son or daughter's partner is not good enough for their little boy or girl. Sometimes they are right.

Many partners have suffered from this affliction and I can state that an overpowering mother is nothing better than a total pain in the arse, and the quicker you put them straight the easier your own life will become. Don't get me wrong, I loved my mother as most people do, but when they start to interfere in your relationships, that is when you should say that enough is enough.

But you need to be very tactful in how you approach this matter, as this can cause a lot of family problems. You must be united as a couple in front of them; do not listen to what others say as you must remember that you make your choice when choosing your partner.

If they treat you well and you are happy together, what the hell does it matter what your parents think? Unless your choice is a drug-dealing mass murderer, or someone who views you as a money machine whilst they sit at home watching the television all day and are out at the pub at night, why should anyone else matter?

The main thing to consider is that your partner respects you and treats you well. After all, your parents have lived their lives and cannot expect to live your life for you. Even though most parents want the very best for their offspring and try to guide you through their own experiences, there are times when you have to stand upon your own feet, but be respectful and explain how you feel...

But not taking parental advice has one exception, and that is: if you are very young and they try to advise you, do not act like a complete idiot. Listen and take notice of what they tell you, as most parents have been in the same situation, then try to decide with their support what will be the best option... If in full-time education then consideration of your future is a must. Take note of what is best for your life ahead as you don't wish to be homeless.

Another factor to take into consideration is cash, or the lack of it. This is a massive argument causer, often leading to breakdowns in any relationship, but it does not stop there.

The list below shows some other factors that destroy relationships before they have had a chance:

Family interference (mothers, fathers, sisters, brothers, whoever).

Male ex-partners and friends keep coming around.

Female ex-partners and friends keep coming around.

Having babies too young or too immature (babies do not cement relationships).

Boys' nights out, often cause jealousy.

Girls' nights out, often cause jealousy.

Friends bitching to one partner about other partners.

Not coming home at the end of an evening out.

Telling lies to partner (this is a big "no-no").

Flirting with opposite sexes in front of you partner.

Lazy partners, whilst you work.

Having a parent who dislikes your partner move in with you, a very big mistake.

Ex-partners who are still close friends.

Going to ex-partners' parties.

It is extremely hard nowadays to start a relationship and know if you will still be together in five years, as there are endless pitfalls to overcome, many of your own making.

The other thing that has amazed me for many years and continues to make me stand back in amazement, is the situation that I call the "Rubber Band Relationship".

This is where a couple endlessly argues, and I do not mean not speaking to each other, I mean standing in the street or a bar or nightclub having a shouting match with each other, going at it big time, swearing and cursing each other and everyone standing around is a little embarrassed to even be near them or in the same area.

These people seem oblivious to the fact that there are others nearby who are thinking, *Why in the hell don't you go somewhere else and do that in private?* Whilst you are standing there waiting for the punches to start flying, they stop and act as if nothing has happened. What the hell? Get a life, will you?

If you are one of these types, please try to show some consideration and argue at home.

To end a rocky relationship solely depends upon being strong enough to say Enough is Enough.

Many people make the wrong decision, and your whole life could depend upon making the right one at this moment. You could save yourself a whole lot of heartache if you are in a stormy relationship, especially if your partner suggests that you should have a child.

This is possibly the stupidest step you could take, as a baby brings with it so many more problems and a hell of a lot of extra stress. So just imagine this: you are already in a rocky unstable relationship and you add a screaming infant who does not sleep well to this already unstable situation, with a pair of immature young people who already scream and shout at each other most of the time they are together. Now ask yourself how you will cope.

The answers are quite simple, and here are just four:

1. Within a short time the boyfriend will leave (this is the guy who said he will always love and stay with you).
2. You and your infant will end up living with your parent, who may I add will already be stressed out, thanks to you.

3. You and your infant will be placed in a centre for single mothers or a bedsit where the infant will continually cry and you will be all alone to deal with it, with very little money and no social life.
4. The endless lack of sleep and continual crying pushes you over the edge and your infant becomes yet another infant death.

I am sorry to have painted such a black picture, but I have known many young women in my previous career who have found themselves going through these stages and who thought that having a child would be easy and would have brought them closer. Big Mistake.

In my past profession, I met many young women aged between fourteen and their early twenties after their partner had persuaded them to have a child and then realised that a baby is a living being who demands a lot of attention and not just another accessory.

Most of them were advised not to do it by family or friends, but thought that they knew best and the boyfriend was such an upstanding young man. This upstanding young man who disappeared as soon as the stuff hit the fan, had his fun and left the girl to deal with it.

One last thing to remember: an infant is not a dolly that you can just pack away, it is a life.

So consideration and common sense is a must when

thinking about pregnancy, as children are not something that can be turned off and packed away in a cupboard.

We have all known some nice girls, but generally, they turn out to be "Just Friends" material. Even if you think that they are the most beautiful, genuine, loving person you have ever known, you are afraid to say anything. Yes, it looks like you have a crush upon this person. What should you do? Well, you have very few choices.

1. Keep quiet and say nothing in the hope that she will fall for you. Some hope.
2. Speak with her and explain how you feel if you are brave enough.
3. Get a friend to have a casual chat and innocently drop in that they think that you would like to ask her out. If she says 'not a chance' at least you will know, but then she may back off from you.
4. Stand back, whilst another man steals any chance you may have with her.

Ask yourself this question.

What do you have to lose?

About now, you will be saying to yourselves, *Why am I so afraid of telling this woman?*

I can assure you that you are not the only one who has

been in this situation, as many people, male and female, find it impossible to approach someone and tell them how they feel. This is normal human reaction, but until you step up and take a chance you will never know.

"The first step is the hardest."

TEA FOR TWO

My wife asked me today if I would like a cup of tea, to which I of course replied, "Please."

Twenty minutes later, I asked her if she had made the tea and she replied, "Oh, I forgot," and then poured the water into my cup and went off to do something else.

A few minutes went by and I went over and removed the teabag and said to her (jokingly), "Oh, your brain cell is overworked."

She replied, "Yes I'm turning into a man."

I just had to laugh as her comeback was brilliant and spontaneous.

Now, I make the tea as well and don't expect her to wait upon me.

7. Sexual & Stuff

Some women suffer from a loss of sexual drive after having a child, so don't just jump to conclusions.

But other times it could be that she may be playing away from home. First find out if the latter is true, as jumping to the wrong conclusion could be a fatal error on your behalf. Without knowing the facts, most men think the worst.

Other reasons are medical grounds, which are no fault of the woman herself, and if so many men fail to understand a woman or consider asking any question as to what is wrong, then it will be their own fault if they get it wrong.

Inadequate sexual function in women is a complex problem that can have many different causes, and it is estimated that up to 40% of women have suffered from some sort of sexual problem in the last year, which may be caused by physical illness, but is often linked to psychological factors.

This is the female equivalent of impotence and is known as Female Sexual Arousal Disorder (FSAD). When men and women become sexually aroused, their genitals become engorged with blood and in women, this normally results in:

An enlargement of the clitoris and surrounding tissues (similar to the male erection).

Secretion of vaginal lubrication.

Relaxation and widening of the vaginal opening permit intercourse.

However, remember this one thing: it does not matter if they are male or female, they do not wear a sign saying, "I am a sexual disease carrier," and this may be the night your life changes for the worse.

A strong grasp of reality would mean that if you meet a female or male in a club or bar and they then jump your bones upon the first night, well, this is a damn good sign that you should be using a condom.

A sure way of stating the obvious is that they are often called easy (this does not just mean women). It is good to practise common sense and use a condom at all times. If you are in the habit of casual sex encounters, you will not know if the person is a carrier of a disease. Your sex partner should ask you to wear a condom if they do not wish to put themselves into a position that could destroy their own life. If they do not demand or suggest safe sex practices, ask yourselves this question: "Do they know something that they are not telling you?"

This is a very serious matter. Consider your future. You may not have one.

Remember the following "Men's Thought for the Day":

"Handle every stressful situation as a dog does – if you can't eat it or hump it, piss on it and walk away."

Men must remember that it is the male who is the one who does most of the chasing, hunting for his sexual fix, whilst the female is looking for the man she can be happy with and trust.

If you happen to meet a female or male and during the early stages of the conversation, they ask you what you do for a job, do you tell her the truth, "I work in a fish and chip shop in Basingstoke," or do you tell her something to make their heart flutter? "I can't say much about what I do" – just keeping them guessing is sometimes a good move. A guy should say, "Let's just talk about you," as that's more interesting.

The strange thing is that no matter what line you give a lady, by the end of the evening she will have turned you inside out and will know everything about you, as most men are not capable of keeping their mouths shut.

Be who you are and say what you feel...

Because of those that matter...

don't mind...

And those that mind...

don't matter.

Sex is something we all enjoy, but remember, forcing someone to have sex is rape. There is a saying that goes as follows: "it is a man's right to ask and a woman's right to refuse".

Questions that I asked both male and females concerning rape and sexual assaults got quite a strong response from both sexes, as both men and women suggested castration as a very good deterrent and some of the men even suggested that the offenders should have "Rapist" tattooed upon their foreheads.

All those that I asked this question to agreed that any sex offences should carry a double life sentence so that offender will never be released back into society and therefore will not be any danger.

A man knows when he does something wrong

As the lady in his life will inform him

Time & Time Again

Now, just think of the following scenario: you meet a woman who you like and later that evening have consensual sex with her, then find yourself being arrested the next day for rape. Sorry to say that this event is fast becoming popular practice within the circles of certain young women, as many of them have realised that there is sizeable compensation payout to be had. As the British law system seems to be stacked in the woman's favour with little or no effort being carried out to prove that they are lying, it can be an easy way of making money as the risk is quite minimal unless they get caught out, then there may be a chance that it will be them spending time behind bars.

Yes, having sex upon a first date can often be harmful to your health in more than one way. Ask yourself, how do you think you would cope if you were arrested for rape and found that you had little or no chance of proving you were innocent?

The other thing that is on the increase is young people failing to protect themselves against sexually transmitted diseases and finding themselves with a nasty life-threatening disease, and this is where spending a little time getting to know someone can help, by allowing you a better insight into what that person is really about. You never know, she may be the one who is just right for you. This works both ways as women can be in similar positions.

Sexual diseases can often destroy lives. Those of you who think, *It will never happen to me*, think again as it often does, and those who practise overlapping sexual relationships are at a greater risk.

As of 2008, sexually transmitted infections (STIs), including HIV, remain one of the most important causes of illness due to infectious diseases among young people (aged between 16 and 24 years old). If left untreated, many STIs can lead to long-term fertility problems (e.g. with chlamydia or gonorrhoea). Infection with HIV or the strains of human papillomavirus (HPV) can cause cervical cancer and can lead to long-term illness or possible death, so make a point to be aware of the dangers if you do not practise "Safe Sex", Be wise, not dead.

The frightening thing about sexually transmitted diseases is having to watch a friend or loved one dying slowly in front of you, simply because they did not listen.

No matter how much we dismiss the fact, it's quite obvious that most men do not enjoy clothes shopping with their partners. As a man walks into a clothes shop to purchase an item, he will generally go straight to the section containing jeans, jumpers, suits or shirt, pick up the items he requires, go to the till, pay and leave.

Now if this is your lady, she will drag you around as many shops as possible for a couple of hours or more and then return to the first shop and pick up the first item that she tried on.

The fact that we men can't control our partners when dealing with clothes shopping is no surprise as we are fully aware that we will bear the brunt of their anger if we speak out, so we stand waiting whilst they grab a handful of items and head for the changing room. This is why shops should have a café or bar in them so us guys can sit and watch a football match or something interesting, whilst our ladies do what they do best, SHOP.

The End

WHY MEN DON'T OFTEN GET DEPRESSED:

Men Are Just Happier People – So Men Say.

What do you expect from such simple creatures?

Your last name stays put.

The garage is all yours. (Are you sure?)

Wedding plans take care of themselves.

Chocolate is just another snack...

You can never be pregnant.

You can wear a white T-shirt to a water park.

You can wear NO shirt to a water park.

Car mechanics tell you the truth.

The world is your urinal.

You never have to drive to another petrol station toilet because this one is just too icky.

You never have strap problems in public.

You are unable to see wrinkles in your clothes.

Everything on your face stays its original colour.

The same hairstyle lasts for years, even decades.

You only have to shave your face and neck.

You can play with toys all your life.

One wallet and one pair of shoes – one colour for all seasons.

You can wear shorts no matter how your legs look.

You can 'do' your nails with a pocket knife.

You have freedom of choice concerning growing a moustache.

You can do Christmas shopping for 25 relatives on December 24th in 25 minutes.

This was surely a man's view

Sorry, ladies, but this is funny.

Supplied by Paul Glover

We always hear "The Rules" from the female side.

Here are the rules from the male side.

THESE ARE THE RULES.

1. MEN ARE NOT MIND READERS.
2. LEARN TO WORK THE TOILET SEAT. YOU'RE A BIG GIRL. IF IT'S UP, PUT IT DOWN. WE NEED IT UP, YOU NEED IT DOWN. YOU DON'T HEAR US COMPLAINING ABOUT YOU LEAVING IT DOWN.
3. CRYING IS BLACKMAIL.

4. ASK FOR WHAT YOU WANT. LET US BE CLEAR ON THIS ONE.

   SUBTLE HINTS DO NOT WORK?

   STRONG HINTS DO NOT WORK?

   OBVIOUS HITS DO NOT WORK?

   JUST SAY IT

5. YES AND NO ARE PERFECTLY ACCEPTABLE ANSWERS TO MOST QUESTIONS.

6. COME TO US WITH A PROBLEM ONLY IF YOU WANT HELP SOLVING IT. THAT'S WHAT WE DO. SYMPATHY IS WHAT YOUR GIRLFRIENDS ARE FOR.

7. ANYTHING WE SAID 6 MONTHS AGO IS INADMISSIBLE IN AN ARGUMENT. ALL COMMENTS BECOME NULL AND VOID AFTER 7 DAYS.

8. IF YOU THINK YOU ARE, YOU PROBABLY ARE. DON'T ASK.

9. IF SOMETHING WE SAID CAN BE INTERPRETED TWO WAYS AND ONE WAY MAKES YOU SAD OR ANGRY, WE MEANT THE OTHER WAY.

10. YOU CAN EITHER ASK US TO DO SOMETHING OR TELL US HOW YOU WANT IT DONE. NOT BOTH.

11. WHENEVER POSSIBLE, PLEASE SAY WHATEVER YOU HAVE TO SAY DURING COMMERCIALS.

12. ALL MEN SEE IN ONLY 16 COLOURS, LIKE WINDOWS DEFAULT SETTINGS: PEACH, FOR EXAMPLE, IS A FRUIT,

NOT A COLOUR, SAME AS PUMPKIN, WHICH IS ALSO A FRUIT. WE HAVE NO IDEA WHAT MAUVE IS.

13. IF WE ASK WHAT IS WRONG AND YOU SAY "NOTHING", WE WILL ACT LIKE NOTHING'S WRONG. WE KNOW YOU ARE LYING, BUT IT IS NOT WORTH THE HASSLE.

14. IF YOU ASK A QUESTION THAT YOU DON'T WANT AN ANSWER TO, EXPECT AN ANSWER YOU DON'T WANT TO HEAR.

15. WHEN WE HAVE TO GO SOMEWHERE, ABSOLUTELY ANYTHING YOU WEAR IS FINE... REALLY.

16. DON'T ASK US WHAT WE'RE THINKING ABOUT UNLESS YOU ARE PREPARED TO DISCUSS TOPICS SUCH AS FOOTBALL OR MOTORSPORT.

17. YOU HAVE ENOUGH CLOTHES.

18. YOU HAVE TOO MANY SHOES.

19. I AM IN SHAPE. ROUND IS A SHAPE.

THANK YOU FOR READING THIS. YES, I KNOW THAT I WILL BE SLEEPING ON THE COUCH AGAIN TODAY, BUT DID YOU KNOW THAT MEN DON'T MIND AS IT FEELS LIKE CAMPING TO THEM?

A BIG THANK YOU TO PAUL GLOVER FOR THIS

A Little Humour

A few for the ladies:

A couple is lying in bed. The man says, 'I am going to make you the happiest woman in the world...'

The woman replies, 'I'll miss you...'

Q: What do you call an intelligent, good-looking, sensitive man?

A: A rumour.

'It's just too hot to wear clothes today,' Jack said as he stepped out of the shower. 'Honey, what do you think the neighbours would think if I mowed the lawn like this?'

'Probably that I married you for your money,' she replied.

Q: What do you call a handcuffed man?

A: Trustworthy.

Q: Why do little boys whine?

A: They are practising being men.

Q: What does it mean when a man is in your bed gasping for breath and calling your name?

A: You did not hold the pillow down long enough.

Q: Why do men whistle when they are sitting on the toilet?

A: It helps them remember which end to wipe.

Q: How do you keep your husband from reading your email?

A: Rename the email folder 'Instruction Manuals'.

Sex in the Dark

There was this couple that had been married for 20 years.

Every time they made love, the husband always insisted on shutting off the light.

Well, after 20 years the wife felt this was ridiculous.

She figured she would break him out of this crazy habit.

So one night, while they were in the middle of a wild, screaming, romantic session, she turned on the lights.

She looked down and saw her husband was holding a battery-operated leisure device... A vibrator! Soft, wonderful and larger than a real one.

She went completely ballistic.

'You impotent bastard,' she screamed at him. 'How could you be lying to me all of these years? You better explain yourself!'

The husband looked her straight in the eyes and said calmly:

'I'll explain the toy... You explain the kids.'

Ass Sizes

I was sent the following email concerning a study carried out asking women how they feel about their asses.

Women's Ass Sizes

10% of women think their ass is too skinny.

30% of women think their ass is too fat.

60% say they don't care, they love him, he is a good man and they wouldn't trade him for the world.

(Must be another woman joke.)

The Wish

A man walking along a Gold Coast beach was deep in prayer. All of a sudden he said out loud, "Lord, grant me one wish."

Suddenly the sky clouded above his head and in a booming voice the Lord said, "Because you have been faithful to me in all ways, I will grant you one wish."

The man said, "Build a bridge to Hawaii, so I can drive over anytime I want to."

The Lord said, "Your request is very materialistic. Think of the logistics of that kind of undertaking. The support required to reach the bottom of the Pacific! The concrete and steel it would take! I can do it, but it is hard for me to justify your desire for worldly things. Take a little more time and think of another wish, a wish you think would honour and glorify me."

The man thought about it for a long time. Finally, he said, "Lord, I have been married and divorced four times. All of my wives said that I am uncaring and insensitive. I wish that I could understand women. I want to know how they feel inside, what they are thinking when they give me the silent treatment, why they cry, what they mean when they say 'nothing' and how I can make a woman truly happy."

After a few minutes, God said, "You want two lanes or four on that bridge?"

Two old ones from many years back

My nookie days are over
My pilot light is out
What used to be my sex appeal
Is now my water spout.

Time was when, on its own accord
From my trousers, it would spring
But now I've got a full-time job
To find the blasted thing.

It used to be embarrassing
The way it would behave
For every single morning
It would stand and watch me shave.

Now as old age approaches
It sure gives me the blues
To see it hang its little head
And watch me tie my shoes...

From 20 to 30, if a man lives right,
It's once in the morning and twice at night,
From 30 to 40, if he still lives right,
Misses the morning and sometimes at night,
From 40 to 50 – is now and then,
From 50 to 60 – is God knows when,
His sporting days are over,
His little light's gone out,
What used to be his Sex Appeal
Is now his Water Spout!

ABOUT THE AUTHOR

Paul has been married to his present wife for 27 years and became an author 15 years ago as a writer of historic refence books, until some comments made by a friend started him upon the research for this book.

Printed in Great Britain
by Amazon